Certificate N

CECILE MILES

Second edition

Pitman Publishing

First published 1965
Reprinted 1966, 1968, 1970
Second edition 1972
Reprinted 1974 1976

PITMAN PUBLISHING LTD
Pitman House, Parker Street, Kingsway, London WC2B 5PB
PO Box 46038, Banda Street, Nairobi, Kenya

PITMAN PUBLISHING PTY LTD
Pitman House, 158 Bouverie Street, Carlton, Victoria 3053, Australia

PITMAN PUBLISHING CORPORATION
6 East 43 Street, New York, NY 10017, USA

SIR ISAAC PITMAN (CANADA) LTD
495 Wellington Street West, Toronto M5V 1G1, Canada

THE COPP CLARK PUBLISHING COMPANY
517 Wellington Street West, Toronto M5V 1G1, Canada

ISBN: 0 273 31524 2

Made in Great Britain at The Pitman Press, Bath
G.3368:55

Preface to the Second Edition

CHANGES in emphasis in the syllabuses for C.S.E. and G.C.E. examinations as well as new developments in man-made fibres and automatic sewing machines have made necessary a new edition of this standard book. A completely new chapter on fabrics has been written, and there is now a section on automatic sewing machines, as well as new material on grooming. Because of the introduction of metrication all working measurements are given in metric units.

Not a great deal has yet been decided about how the cloth and paper pattern industries will go metric. So far as we know at present, pattern sizes will remain the same, though measurements for bust, waist, hips, etc., will be given in centimetres.

Here is a table with these measurements given in inches and centimetres—

Size	10		12		14		16		18	
	inches	cms	inches	cms	inches	cms	inches	cms	inches	cms
Bust	32½	83	34	86	36	91	38	99	40	102
Waist	24	61	25½	65	27	68	29	74	31	79
Hips	34½	88	36	91	38	97	40	102	42	107

The seam allowance on paper patterns is likely to be 1·5 cms instead of the present ⅝″. Fabrics will continue to be produced for some time to come in the widths we are used to, but inches will be converted to the nearest whole centimetre. Here are the most commonly used fabric widths given in both Imperial and Metric measurements.

Imperial		*Metric*
36″	=	91 cms
45″	=	114 cms
54″	=	137 cms
60″	=	152 cms

Soon (by about 1975) you will have to ask for cloth by the metre instead of the yard. Here is a conversion table giving the most commonly required dress-making lengths both in yards and metres.

Yds	m	Yds	m	Yds	m	Yds	m	Yds	m	Yds	m	Yds	m	Yds	m
⅛	0·15	¼	0·25	⅜	0·35	½	0·50	⅝	0·60	¾	0·70	⅞	0·80	1	0·95
1⅛	1·05	1¼	1·15	1⅜	1·30	1½	1·40	1⅝	1·50	1¾	1·60	1⅞	1·75	2	1·85
2⅛	1·95	2¼	2·10	2⅜	2·20	2½	2·30	2⅝	2·40	2¾	2·55	2⅞	2·65	3	2·75
3⅛	2·90	3¼	3·00	3⅜	3·10	3½	3·25	3⅝	3·35	3¾	3·45	3⅞	3·55	4	3·70
4⅛	3·80	4¼	3·90	4⅜	4·00	4½	4·15	4⅝	4·25	4¾	4·35	4¾	4·50	5	4·60
5⅛	4·70	5¼	4·85	5⅜	4·95	5½	5·05	5⅝	5·15	5¾	5·30	5⅞	5·40	6	5·50
6⅛	5·65	6¼	5·75	6⅜	5·85	6½	5·95	6⅝	6·10	6¾	6·20	6⅞	6·30	7	6·45

Throughout *Certificate Needlework* measurements have been given in metric only as we thought it would be easier to learn the metric system by forgetting all about inches and thinking entirely in metric.
Remember—

1″ = 2·54 cms   1 cm = 0·4″
1′ = 30·50 cms   1 m = 1·1 yds
1 yd = 91 cms

Contents

Introductory

THERE are very few occupations that can give the same degree of pleasure and satisfaction as sewing. Embroidery can help you to express your interest and skill in design and colour, and the making of garments that reflect your own taste and ideas may be a real joy.

Needlework is an ancient craft, and may be about fifty thousand years old. "Needles" were once made from fish-bones and thorns, "thread" was made of animal sinew and the "fabrics" were skins and furs. Obviously sewing was not easy with such primitive tools and difficult materials, and the results must have left a lot to be desired. But man's ingenuity gradually enabled him to make new materials and tools, and the making of garments became less difficult.

Steel needles were not invented until about 1670, which is, therefore, an important date in the history of sewing.

The first scissors were a kind of crude shears, invented by a shepherd for clipping sheep, and it was not until a cheap method of making steel was discovered in 1856 that scissors became plentiful and cheap.

An important development was made possible by the invention of the sewing-machine. Experiments had been made with chain-stitching machines round about 1830, but suitable, cheap materials were scarce and it was another twenty years before the supply of materials was more favourable and the lock-stitch machine was invented. This was a wonderful step forward. These early machines would, however, seem very crude and primitive to us, when compared with the machines with which we are familiar today.

Linen was the first fabric made. The flax from which it was spun and woven was used in Egypt as early as 6000 B.C. whereas the earliest records of wool being used came from the Middle East, about 4000 B.C. Cotton cloth was made in India in 3000 B.C. and China gave the world silk in 2700 B.C. The spinning and weaving was all done by hand and was a slow and tedious process, but in the 1700's the industry began to be mechanized and has since developed into one of the most important industries in the modern world.

Needlework is a craft. This implies that skill and dexterity are needed to achieve good results. But interest and application will enable most people to learn it. The sense of achievement experienced on the completion of a well-made, wearable garment is indeed worth working for.

I
Equipment

GETTING the right tools for the job is the first step towards success, and the care of them is also of great importance.

TOOLS

Needlework tools can be divided into three groups: your own personal work-box tools, workroom equipment, and pressing equipment.

1. PERSONAL TOOLS: THE CONTENTS OF YOUR WORKBOX

Needles

An assortment is needed, and the following would be adequate for a wide range of work—

Sharps—medium length, used for general sewing. Sizes 1–12.
Straws—long, millinery needles, useful for tacking. Sizes 1–12.
Betweens—short, used for fine work, buttonholes, etc. Sizes 1–12.
Darners—long, large eye to take wool or thick thread. Sizes 1–12.
Crewel—medium length, long eye, used for embroidery. Sizes 1–12.
Tapestry—blunt point, long eye, used for embroidery on canvas. Sizes 13–26.

The higher the number, the finer the needle; numbers 6, 7, 8 are the most useful. A tapestry needle No. 19 is equivalent to a sewing needle No. 1.

FABRIC	NEEDLE SIZE
Fine fabrics—lawn, voile, silk, lace	Nos. 8 or 9
Medium fabrics—poplin, piqué, gingham, fine woollens	No. 7
Heavy fabrics—denim, tweed, furnishing fabrics	Nos. 5 or 6
Synthetics—nylon, Terylene	Nos. 8 or 9

Pins

Dressmaker's steel pins are best, because they are smooth and sharp, and make very little mark on fabrics. They must be kept away from moisture, to prevent them rusting.

Tape-measure

A strong and clearly marked tape-measure is necessary. A stiff end is useful for measuring hems and tucks.

Thimble

It should be well fitting and comfortable.

Scissors

For cutting out, the minimum length of the blades should be 15 cms. Longer blades should be used for heavy materials. Embroidery scissors should be small and sharp-pointed. A spare pair of medium-size scissors is useful for snipping threads and cutting paper. Never use good scissors for the latter purpose.

Threads

It is important to use thread of the correct thickness and colour for the material. There is a general rule that the thread used should be of the same material as that in the fabric: cotton thread for cotton fabrics, silk thread for silk fabrics, and synthetic threads for synthetic fabrics. The finer the material the finer and softer the sewing-thread should be.

Sewing-cotton is obtainable in a variety of thicknesses and colours. Mercerized cotton is available in a limited number of thicknesses, but a large range of colours. It is not as strong as cotton but has a good appearance because it is glossy. Sewing-silk is strong and elastic and is obtainable in a good range of colours. Synthetic thread is very fine, strong and elastic. It washes, dries and wears in a similar manner to synthetic materials, but there is only a limited range of colours.

A reel of thread that looks a shade darker than the material will work in better than a lighter shade.

Use cotton 40 or buttonhole twist for sewing on buttons.

Tacking-cotton should always be used for tacking because it is soft and easily broken, and can be pulled out without damaging the material. Sylko gives the best results when working buttonholes.

FABRIC	THREAD
Very fine cottons—lawn, voile, muslin	Cotton 80–100. Sylko 60
Medium cottons—shirtings, poplin, gingham	Cotton 60. Sylko 40
Heavy cottons—calico, drill, sailcloth	Cotton 40
Silks, rayon, jersey, woollens	Sewing silk
Synthetics—nylon, Terylene	Trylko (Terylene thread)

2. WORKROOM EQUIPMENT

A cutting-out table of a convenient height, and large enough to take a complete pattern lay.

A full-length mirror.

A sewing machine of the type most suitable for your purpose—hand or electric, portable or table model, or treadle.

A wardrobe for hanging unfinished garments.

Drawers for storing equipment.

A dress-stand made to your own measurements or an adjustable one.

3. PRESSING EQUIPMENT

An iron that is heat controlled.

A skirt-board, padded and with a washable cover.

A sleeve-board also padded with a washable cover.

A padded roller for pressing seams (*see* Fig. 1).

Tailor's cushion for pressing darts and curved seams (*see* Fig. 2).

Pressing-cloths.

FIG. 1   FIG. 2

CARE OF EQUIPMENT

Cleanliness is very important. All covers should be washed regularly; pressing-cloths should be washed and thoroughly rinsed after use. If pins have to be collected from the floor, rub them in a dry cloth before returning them to your pin-box. The iron should be kept clean and polished and the flex renewed if it shows signs of fraying. Scissors should be kept in a leather or plastic case to protect the points.

As instructed by the booklet, your machine should be cleaned and oiled according to the amount of use it is given. A pipe-cleaner is useful for clearing away the lint and fluff that gathers round the shuttle. Use the oil recommended by the makers, and store the machine away from dust, damp and excessive heat.

USING THE SEWING MACHINE

Study the instruction booklet and learn the names of the different parts of the machine and their uses (*see* Fig. 3). Make sure that you can thread the machine correctly (*see* Figs. 4 and 5). Learn to recognize faults in the stitching and their likely causes (*see* Fig. 6). Test the machine on double material. Watch the edge of the foot, not the needle, for straight stitching. Sit comfortably, in a good light, and concentrate on your work. Keep the bulk of the work to the left of the foot. If using a hand machine, never let anyone else turn the handle for you.

AUTOMATIC SEWING MACHINES

The modern automatics are quite easy to use and control. Time spent studying the instruction manual so that you thoroughly understand the threading of the machine is an important first step. Then practice using the machine to do straight stitching; if you use the reduction gear you will discover that you can machine with greater precision than ever before.

The booklet given with the machine gives clear instructions on how to care for the machine. There is also a list of faults giving the causes and how to correct them.

Read and follow the advice given about the choice of thread for the particular job that you are doing; this is important and makes a great difference to the result.

These machines can do a great many time-saving things—

1. Zig-zag stitching is quick and easy and takes the boredom out of endless seam neatening; the stitch can be adjusted to suit any fabric.

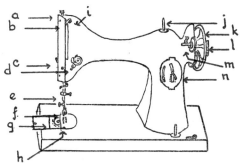

FIG. 3

(a)	Presser bar	(h)	Feed plate
(b)	Thread take-up lever	(i)	Thread guide
(c)	Presser foot lifter	(j)	Spool pin
(d)	Tension discs	(k)	Balance wheel
(e)	Needle clamp	(l)	Stop motion screw
(f)	Presser foot	(m)	Bobbin winder
(g)	Bobbin and shuttle	(n)	Stitch regulator

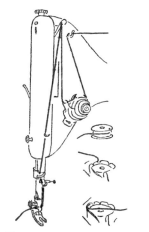

Threading the machine
FIG. 4

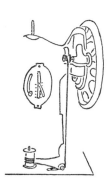

Winding the bobbin
FIG. 5

 Correct stitch

 Top tension too strong

 Top tension too weak

FIG. 6

2. The three way zig-zag is invaluable when stitching jersey and other stretch fabrics.

3. Blind stitching is a quicker way of securing a hem than slip hemming by hand.

4. With practice it is possible to do very presentable buttonholes in a fraction of the time it takes to work them by hand.

5. The zipper foot is a great help when putting in a zip fastener or using corded piping.

6. The machine can be set to do a number of decorative stitches which are useful when making children's clothes and household articles.

7. Darning and mending can also be done quickly and neatly on a variety of fabrics.

2
Fabrics

THE study of fabrics is both interesting and rewarding and, although it is a very large subject, the following pages should give enough information for the recognition of most materials. The outline of manufacture has been described in brief in all cases, but the processes which have most influence on the final appearance of the fabrics are given in more detail.

Actual samples are much more informative than photographs, and students should collect examples of as many different types of fabric as possible, naming them and giving their uses. It helps if two adjacent edges of each sample are frayed out so that the type of yarn used and the number of threads per square centimetre in both warp and weft are easily seen.

Fabrics may be divided into two sections.

1. *Natural*—from animal and vegetable sources.
2. *Man-made*—(*a*) from regenerated cellulose and cellulose derivatives.
   (*b*) synthetically produced by the chemical treatment of certain raw materials.

NATURAL FIBRES

COTTON

Cotton is still the most widely used and useful of all fibres. It is very versatile and retains its popularity in spite of the invention of man-made fibres because of the scientific discoveries and up-to-date methods of the Lancashire cotton industry.

The Properties of Cotton Fabrics

Cotton is strong, which makes it hardwearing and suitable for work clothes, but it can also be fine and delicate enough for lingerie. None of its strength is lost when it is wet and this makes it easy to launder; it can be scrubbed, boiled and bleached and it is not harmed by soaps and soda (alkalies). It can be pressed with a hot iron either steam or dry.

Cotton is absorbent and the moisture evaporates fairly quickly which makes it comfortable and cool to wear as underwear, sportswear and for clothes worn in hot climates.

It is relatively inexpensive.
It dyes well either as yarn or fabric.
It is not harmed by moth.
It is inflammable and burns away to a small amount of grey ash.
It creases easily.

Cotton finishes

A "finish" is the name given to any one of a number of different processes to which a fabric may be subjected in order to improve its performance in wear. There is a special section describing each finish in more detail on page 26.

Finishes often applied to cotton are as follows—

Shrink-resistance—(Rigmel or Sanforized).
Crease-resistance—(Tebilized, Carefree, Minicare).
Flame-resistance—(Proban).
Stiffening—(Trubenized).
Sheen—(Mercerized, Everglaze).
Permanent press or non-iron—(Tootapress, Fixaform, Micral).
Embossing—gives a raised pattern.
Tutoring—gives a puckered appearance.
Brushing—gives a fluffy surface for warmth.

The Origin and a Brief Outline of the Manufacture of Cotton Fabrics

The cotton plant grows in the tropical and sub-tropical regions of the world, and the fibres are obtained from the seed pod or bol of the plant. The quality varies; the cotton grown in the West Indies (Sea Island Cotton) and in Egypt and the Sudan (Egyptian Cotton) has longer, finer and silkier fibres than that grown in America and India.

Cotton is gathered by hand or machine and fed into a ginning machine which discards the seeds, stalks and leaves; it also separates the very short fibres which are useless for making into cotton yarn. These very short fibres are called cotton linters and are used for making rayon. The fibres are then baled ready for shipping.

When the bales reach the mills they are broken down and the mass of fibres is beaten and combed, teased and fluffed up by currents of air. More of the impurities are removed at the same time. The mass of fibres now looks like a large sheet of cotton wool and is called a lap. A scutching machine loosens the lap by passing it through fluted rollers. This also makes the remaining impurities drop out.

Next the lap is passed through a carding machine which pulls and combs it into loose ropes called slivers. Six slivers are twisted together and drawn out to the thickness of one in a draw-frame. This process is repeated several times making the sliver thinner each time until it is about the thickness of coarse string. It is now called a roving and is wound onto wooden bobbins ready for spinning.

The spinning process will be dealt with under a separate heading (*see* page 20).

LINEN

Linen is the oldest of all fabrics and although it is similar to cotton in that they are both made from cellulose, linen is smoother and has a natural gloss. It is more expensive than cotton mainly because it has not been mass-produced to the extent that cotton has.

The Properties of Linen Fabrics

Linen is very strong and hard-wearing, which has made it very popular for household articles; it is also used for awnings, tents and tarpaulins.

It tailors well and so is popular for ladies' and men's suits.

It has good wet strength and will stand up to frequent machine washing.

It is not harmed by high temperatures and is used extensively in hospitals because it can be boiled and heat-sterilized.

It is very absorbent which makes it suitable for glass cloths, towelling and tropical suiting.

Its natural sheen makes it perfect for high quality table linen.

Because the long fibres have no twist in them, linen has no elasticity and continual creasing in the same place will make it split.

It is inflammable and flares up leaving a grey ash.

It takes dye well.

It creases and frays easily.

Linen finishes

> Crease-resistance.
> Flame-proofing.
> Water-proofing.
> Beetling—gives extra sheen to table linen.

The Origin and a Brief Outline of the Manufacture of Linen Fabrics

Linen fibres are obtained from the stems of the flax plant which grows fairly easily in temperate climates. The bundles of fibres run the whole length of the stem but they are jointed which gives each fibre the appearance of a bamboo cane and causes the finished yarn to be of slightly uneven thickness.

First, the plants are harvested and left to dry and the seeds and leaves are removed by a process called rippling. The fibres are separated from the unwanted parts of the stem by another process called retting, which is a method of rotting away the woody and fleshy parts but leaving the long fibres unharmed. These fibres are then dried and put through the scutching machine which, as we have learnt, breaks down and removes impurities. Then the hackling machine combs, straightens and removes short and broken fibres. The long fibres are formed into slivers which are drawn and twisted in the same manner as cotton ready to be spun into yarn.

The best quality yarn is made from the longest fibres. The short fibres or tow are used for poorer quality fabrics and twine.

Wool

The continuing popularity of woollen fabrics is well deserved, its inherent good qualities have always outweighed its shortcomings such as its tendency to shrink and its attraction for moth grubs. But these problems have now been overcome, and, moreover, woollen fabrics can be permanently creased, which makes wool a desirable fabric for many purposes.

The Properties of Woollen Fabrics

Wool is warm because each fibre has a natural crimp which in the finished fabric traps pockets of air. This warmth makes it comfortable both for outer and under clothing.

Wool is absorbent and can hold quite a lot of moisture without losing its warmth, which makes it comfortable to wear next to the skin.

Woollen garments keep their shape because of the elasticity of the crimped fibres.

If wool is washed it must be done with great care because it felts easily. Heavy woollen garments should be dry cleaned.

Wool will burn, but it does not flare up as cotton and linen do.

Woollen finishes

Shrink-resistance—this treatment lengthens the life of woollen garments. Labels to look for are Dylan, Epilox, B.D.A.

Moth-proofing—the fabric is treated with a harmless chemical which is unpleasant to moth grubs. Labels to look for are Mitin and Dielmoth.

Permanent creasing—makes frequent pressing unnecessary.

Shower-proofing—a finish used on worsted fabrics for raincoats.

The Origin and a Brief Outline of the Manufacture of Woollen Fabrics

Wool is obtained mainly from the fleeces of sheep, Merino sheep giving the best quality because the fibres are long and fine. Australia and New Zealand are two of the main wool producing countries.

The fleeces are very greasy and dirty and have to be thoroughly washed and rinsed before the long fibres can be separated from the short ones. The short fibres are used to make woollen yarns which are hairy, and the long fibres are made into worsted yarns which are smooth and fine. The short fibres are carded, which means that they are mixed up until they lie in all directions in a thin layer. This is then divided into slivers or loose ropes which are doubled, pulled and twisted into rovings ready for spinning. The long fibres are combed to make them lie parallel with one another, divided into slivers, drawn, twisted and combed again. Six slivers are twisted together and drawn into a fine roving ready for spinning.

SILK

Silk is a luxury fabric of great beauty, and its strength and good wearing qualities offset to some extent its high cost.

The Properties of Silk

Strength—in spite of its fineness silk is almost equal to nylon in strength.

Elasticity—this adds to its strength and gives it the very desirable quality of good crease recovery.

Warmth—silk feels warm against the skin which makes it very comfortable for underwear.

Absorbent—silk will absorb a fair amount of moisture without loosing its feeling of warmth. This makes it comfortable to wear next to the skin.

A good insulator—this quality makes it suitable for clothing in all seasons and climates.

Non-irritant—it can be worn next to the most delicate skins.

It has a beautiful natural sheen.

It can be either soft or stiff.

Care must be taken when laundering. Mild detergents are more suitable than soap.

Silk finishes

Dyeing—silk takes dye well either as yarn or piece goods.

Printing—screen printing is the method most often used.

Weighting—not all silks are weighted, but when fullness and body are required the silk filament is made to absorb metallic salts.

The Origin and a Brief Outline of the Manufacture of Silk Fabrics

The silk industry originated in China, but now Japan, India, Italy and France also export silk.

Silk is obtained from the cocoon spun by the caterpillar of the silk moth. The cultivated silk moth is *Bombyx mori* which feeds on mulberry leaves. Its cocoon is composed of a continuous filament of silk which is held in place by a gummy substance called sericin making it into quite a firm structure.

The chrysalis inside the cocoon must be killed before it is ready to emerge to prevent it from breaking the cocoon. It is killed either by steam or electricity. The cocoons are put into hot water to unwind the silk filament. The hot water melts the sericin thus making it possible, with the aid of a brush, to release the silk filaments. The silk threads are extremely fine, therefore five or seven cocoons are unwound together and the sericin hardens them into a single thread. This process is known as reeling and the resulting thread is called raw silk.

The raw silk is then subjected to a process called throwing which means doubling and twisting it into a more substantial yarn known as nett silk. At this stage the silk yarn is still stiff with gum and if it is to be yarn dyed the gum must be removed by boiling in soapy water. Some silks are woven before the gum is removed and then piece dyed.

There is always a lot of silk left on the cocoons after the filament has broken; this is known as waste silk, and after it has been degummed it is cut into even lengths of about 15 cms, combed, put through rollers to form a lap, divided into slivers, pulled and twisted into rovings which are spun into a yarn called spun or schappe silk.

Fabrics made from spun silk are soft and wear well but have less sheen than fabrics made from nett silk.

Sewing threads are made from both nett and spun yarns, the spun being the easier to use because it is less slippery but it is also less elastic.

There is another popular type of silk often called Wild Silk. It is the product of the Tussah and Munga moths which feed on oak leaves. The fabric has a coarser and uneven appearance but is crisp, strong and hardwearing. Shanrung, Pongee and Tussore are some of the names given to these silks.

MAN-MADE FIBRES

Regenerated Cellulose and Cellulose Derivatives

There are three types of fibre made from regenerated cellulose—

1. *Viscose rayon*   2. *Acetate rayon*   3. *Triacetate rayon*

Rayon was the first of the man-made fibres, and because the resulting fabric was soft and shiny it was called Artificial Silk, but as the quality improved and the variety developed it was considered to be an important fabric in its own right. It is neither as strong nor as beautiful as silk, but it is a great deal cheaper. It is obtainable both as filament yarn, which makes a smooth and glossy fabric, and as staple yarn, which makes a dull and more bulky fabric. The latter is often used as a blend with natural fibres.

VISCOSE RAYON

Properties

Absorbent.

A good heat conductor, but feels cold to the touch.

Washes well but is less strong wet than dry and should not be wrung.

A cool iron is necessary as the fabric will stand very little heat.

Soft and drapes well but creases easily, care should be taken not to crease it when it is wet.

Moth-and mildew-proof.

Inflammable—it burns like cotton.

Finishes Applied to Viscose Rayon

Flame-proofing.

Crease-resistance.

Brushing—to give warmth.

Crimping—to give elasticity.

Dyeing and printing.

The Origin and a Brief Outline of the Manufacture of Viscose Rayon

Viscose rayon is made from wood pulp which is subjected to a series of chemical processes using carbon disulphide and caustic soda until it becomes a syrup-like fluid which is forced through the tiny holes in a spinneret (*see* Fig. 7) into a bath of sulphuric acid which hardens the continuous filaments. These filaments are then washed and wound onto spools ready for weaving or knitting. If staple yarn is required the filaments are gathered into bundles and cut into short, even lengths.

THE SPINNERET

The spinneret (*see* Fig. 7) is used in the manufacture of all man-made fibres and as the diagram shows it is a nozzle with very fine holes through which the syrup-like fluid is extruded, forming a continuous filament.

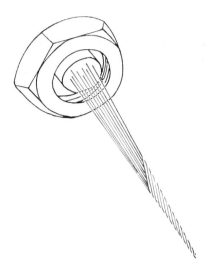

FIG. 7

ACETATE RAYON

The Properties of Acetate Rayon

Absorbent.

Slightly warmer to handle than viscose rayon.

Drapes well.

Good crease recovery when dry, but care must be taken not to crease when wet.

Launders well but iron heat must be low.

Moth-and mildew-proof.

Inflammable.

Certain cleaning fluids are harmful, therefore it must be labelled before cleaning.

Finishes Applied to Acetate Rayon

Flame-proofing.

Crease-resistance.

Embossing—to give surface interest.

Brushing—to give warmth.

The Origin and a Brief Outline of the Manufacture of Acetate Rayon

Acetate rayon is made from cotton linters which are the waste cotton fibres too short for spinning.

The fibres are dissolved in acetic acid, matured, dried and mixed with acetone to become a syrupy fluid ready to be forced through the tiny holes in a spinneret. The filaments harden in warm air and are wound onto spools ready for weaving or knitting. If staple yarn is required the filaments are cut into short lengths and subjected to the same processes of carding, drawing, twisting and spinning as cotton fibres.

TRIACETATE RAYON (TRICEL)

The Properties of Tricel (Trade name by Courtaulds Ltd)

Tricel is much less absorbent than either viscose or acetate rayon, therefore it will drip dry and needs very little ironing.

Needs special dyes because of its non-absorbency.

It will stand more heat than other rayons.

Thermoplastic—it can be permanently pleated and embossed.

Resists creasing.

Finishes Applied to Tricel

Crease-resistance.

Permanent pleating.

Dyeing and printing.

The Origin and a Brief Outline of the Manufacture of Tricel

Tricel is a development of acetate rayon. It is made from cotton linters following similar processes to acetate rayon, except that instead of acetic acid Methylene chloride is used to form the spinning fluid. The filaments harden in warm air and if staple yarn is needed the same processes are followed as those used for acetate rayon.

Synthetics

There are three groups of synthetic fibres each of which is different, but the method of manufacture in each case is similar.

1. *Polyamides*—Nylon, Bri-nylon, Celon, Enkalon.
2. *Polyesters*—Terylene, Dacron.
3. *Acrylics*—Acrilan, Courtelle, Orlon.

POLYAMIDES

Nylon is an American invention but Bri-nylon and Celon are the British equivalent, Enkalon is Dutch.

The Properties of Nylon

Very strong with outstanding resistance to abrasion.
Natural elasticity—the reason why it is used for making stockings.
Non-absorbent and cold to the touch.
Lightweight.
Thermoplastic.
Immune to moth and mildew damage.
Easy to launder—will drip dry and needs little ironing.
Electrostatic—makes it attract dirt.
Strong sunlight tends to rot and discolour it.
It melts and shrinks from a naked flame.
Care must be taken to use a cool iron when pressing during the making of a garment.

Finishes Applied to Nylon Yarns and Fabrics

Bulking—to give softness and warmth.
Crimping—to give extra elasticity for making stretch fabrics.
Texturing—to give a fluffy surface.
Permanent pleating and embossing.
Water-proofing.

The Origin and a Brief Outline of the Manufacture of Nylon

The materials used are Benzine from coal, Oxygen and Nitrogen from air, and Hydrogen from water.

These materials are combined and heated to form a thick fluid which when cooled becomes a hard white sheet called polymer, which is broken into polymer chips. The chips are subjected to considerable heat to melt them to a syrupy liquid which is forced through a spinneret. The fine silky filaments are air-cooled and wound onto spools.

The next process is to draw or stretch them to four times their original length, which results in a very fine smooth yarn of considerable strength and elasticity.

For staple yarn the filaments are combined and cut into short lengths ready for spinning by the same methods as those used for cotton.

POLYESTERS

Terylene is a British invention but America makes the same fabric calling it Dacron.

The Properties of Terylene

Very strong with a high resistance to abrasion, giving excellent wearing qualities.
Crease-resistant.
Does not shrink or stretch.
Thermoplastic.
Moth- and mildew-proof
Resists strong sunlight, which makes it popular for curtains.
Fabrics made from staple fibres are warm to the touch.
Non-absorbent.
Melts when exposed to a naked flame.
Must not be boiled.
Electrostatic.

Finishes Applied to Terylene Yarns and Fabrics

Crimping and stretch twisting—to make elastic yarns.
Bulking—for softness and warmth.
Texturing—to make it fluffy and comfortable.
Permanent pleating and creasing.

The Origin and a Brief Outline of the Manufacture of Terylene

The raw materials used are Ethylene Glycol and Terephthalic acid, which are products of the petroleum industry.

The chemicals are processed to form a thick fluid which solidifies when cooled, cut into chips which are melted to form the spinning fluid and forced through a spinneret. The continuous filament is air-cooled, stretched to several times its original length and wound onto bobbins ready for weaving or knitting.

For staple yarn the coarser filaments are stretched or drawn in groups, crimped, heatset and cut into short lengths ready for spinning.

ACRYLICS

Courtelle is a British fabric, Acrilan and Orlon are American fabrics.

The Properties of Acrilan and Courtelle

Soft, lightweight and warm.
Strong and hardwearing.
Non-irritant.
Crease-resistant.
Thermoplastic.
Electrostatic.
Melts and shrinks from a naked flame.
Washes easily and drip dries.
Will only take a cool iron and steam must not be used.

Finishes Applied to Acrylic Yarns and Fabrics.

Bulking for knitwear.
Permanent pleating and creasing.

The Origin and a Brief Outline of the Manufacture of Acrylic Fabrics

Acrylic fibres are made mainly from a substance called Acrylonitrile, which is obtained from coal carbonization, and natural gas from oil wells.

The processes followed are similar to those used in making other man-made fibres and result in a hard white sheet which is broken up and dissolved into a spinning fluid, after which it is put through the spinneret to form a continuous filament yarn. Acrylic yarn is never used in filament form but crimped and cut into short lengths ready for spinning.

It is the crimping of the yarn that makes it so like wool in warmth and appearance.

Mixtures and Blends

A MIXTURE

A fabric woven or knitted with two or more different yarns is known as a mixture. The two yarns may be twisted together or used separately as warp and weft. It is usually possible to distinguish the two yarns, particularly at the cut or torn edge.

A BLEND

When a yarn has been spun from a blend of two or more different fibres it is known as a blend. This has resulted in a whole new range of fabrics which combine the properties of all the fibres used giving great variety of texture and colour effects. Most blends are labelled as to their content because the correct laundering and care of a garment depends on knowing what it is made of.

SPINNING

All staple fibres, natural and man-made, have to be spun to be made into yarn.

This process first draws out and twists the rovings into yarn, thus making it finer and stronger, then winds it onto spindles. There is a great variety of yarns and it is the yarn that is used that accounts for the appearance and character of the finished fabric.

If long and very fine fibres are used (e.g. Sea Island cotton, linen, worsted and man-made staple fibres) a very fine, smooth yarn is produced which is suitable for voiles, lawns and worsted suitings.

The shorter the fibres are the less fine and smooth the yarn will be, and this yarn is used for medium-weight dress and household articles.

Folded Yarns

Folding means twisting anything from two to six single yarns of the same thickness together; this adds greatly to the strength of the yarn. A folded yarn of the same thickness as a single yarn is also much stronger. The amount of twist given to the yarn in the folding process can alter the appearance of the yarn and add to its elasticity.

Most clothing fabrics are made from "two fold" yarn, the heavier yarns being used for household and industrial purposes.

Many fancy yarns are produced during the spinning and folding.

Slubbed yarn is formed during the spinning, the yarn having been allowed to thicken at even intervals.

Spiral yarns are formed during the folding process. The twist is made more obvious sometimes by folding yarns of two different colours together.

Looped yarns are made during the folding process by making one yarn form small loops at even intervals.

Snarled yarn is a mass of tiny twisted loops and is usually used in conjunction with a plain yarn.

MAKING YARN INTO FABRIC

There are two ways in which yarn can be made into a fabric—

1. *Weaving*—the interlacing of the warp yarns (lengthwise) with weft yarns (across the fabric).
2. *Knitting*—the interlocking of rows of loops (Jersey fabrics).

Weaving

Weaving is done on a loom and is an entirely mechanical process. You can recognize different fabrics if you know (a) what yarn was used (b) the number of threads per square centimetre (c) the type of weave that was used.

PLAIN WEAVE

This is the simplest and strongest weave in which the weft threads go over and under alternate warp threads (*see* Fig. 8). The more threads per square centimetre used in both warp and weft, the stronger and firmer the fabric will

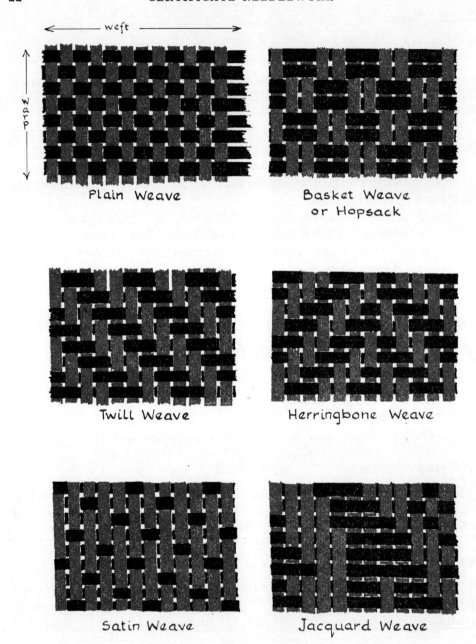

Plain Weave

Basket Weave
or Hopsack

Twill Weave

Herringbone Weave

Satin Weave

Jacquard Weave

FIG. 8

be. The coarser the yarn used the heavier the fabric will be. If a completely even fabric is required all the threads must be of equal thickness, and the number of threads per square centimetre must be the same for both warp and weft. When making dress fabrics the thread count and the thickness of the threads is often varied according to the effect required. Poplin has a fine weft rib which means that the weft thread is slightly thicker than the warp thread. Plain weave is used for most sheer fabrics but the thread count is smaller and very fine yarn is used. Hopsack is also plain weave but two weft threads go over and under two alternate warp threads (*see* Fig. 8).

TWILL WEAVE

This weave is easily recognizable by the diagonal lines on the surface of the cloth; it produces a soft fabric which is rather more bulky than plain weave fabrics (*see* Fig. 8).

The weft thread passes over and under two alternate warp threads but moves forward one warp thread in each row. Variations of this weave are Herringbone (*see* Fig. 8) and Houndstooth. Drill, gaberdine and denim are typical examples of twill weave.

SATIN WEAVE

This weave (*see* Fig. 8) gives a soft and glossy fabric because the warp threads "float" over a number of weft threads. Very fine yarn is used and the thread count is large. The weft thread goes over one and under four warp threads moving two threads to the right in each row.

Sateen is a variation of satin weave but it is the weft threads that "float". Slightly coarser threads are used and the fabric is mainly used for linings.

JACQUARD WEAVE

A very complicated loom is used for this so that very elaborate designs can be woven in self or contrasting colours. Brocades, damasks and tapestries are all examples of Jacquard weave (*see* Fig. 8).

VELVET WEAVE

Velvets are woven on a special loom which involves having the normal warp and weft plus a second warp which interlocks with the ground fabric and forms loops by passing over wires; as the wires are drawn out they cut the loops thus forming the pile (*see* Fig. 9).

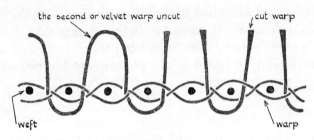

Velvet Weave

FIG. 9

Terry towelling is made in the same way but the loops are left uncut.

Knitted Fabrics

The main characteristics of knitted or jersey fabrics are their elasticity, comfort and crease resistance. All fibres, with the exception of linen, are made into fabrics by this method, and they vary from the almost sheer silk and nylon jerseys used for lingerie and nightwear to the heavy knit cardigans and coats.

There are two main types of jersey fabric—

1. *Weft knitting* which is very like hand knitting in appearance but much finer, has similar variations of stitch including rib and an interlocking stitch which produces Double Jersey (*see* Fig. 10).

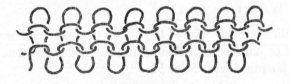

Knitting

FIG. 10

2. *Warp knitting* which is a more complicated process using several threads at once producing a very stable fabric which tends to be ladderproof. Milanese is knitted on a warp knitting machine and that does not run. Openwork and lacey designs are also produced by this method.

Crimplene, which is knitted from bulked filament terylene and often has a Jacquard design on the right side, is a very stable fabric.

DYEING

Modern dyes are excellent, and only those used on very cheap fabrics are not colour-fast.

There are two ways of dyeing cloth.

Sometimes the yarn is dyed before it is woven into a fabric; this is particularly the case when a woven check or striped design is intended and different coloured yarns are needed for the weaving process. Dyeing the yarn can give added richness and depth of colour to any fabric.

The other method is to piece dye the fabric after it has been finished in other ways.

The absorbent fabrics take dye better than the non-absorbent ones, so chemists have had to find new dyes for some of the man-made fabrics. The dye can be added to the spinning fluid before it is extruded from the spinneret; this gives the fabric a good depth of colour.

PRINTING

The dye used for printing designs on fabrics is not liquid but paste. There are three methods—

BLOCK PRINTING

This is the oldest method, it is slow and expensive and rarely used except on luxury silk headscarves. It is costly because of the time needed to hand carve the design on a separate wood block for each colour being used. It is a skilled process done entirely by hand; the blocks are pressed onto a dye pad and then on the material.

SCREEN PRINTING

This method of printing is very like stencilling and a separate screen is needed for each colour. When this method was done by hand it was slow and only used on expensive fabrics but it has now been automated and a great many fabrics are labelled screen printed. The process is a good one giving variety and richness to the design.

ROLLER PRINTING

This process is used when thousands of yards of the same design are needed. The design is engraved on copper rollers; a separate roller is used for each colour. The roller picks up the paste dye and impresses the design onto the fabric as it is fed into the machine. The method is quick and accurate.

FABRIC FINISHES

A finish is a treatment applied to a fabric or yarn to improve its appearance and performance. When buying material, it is worth while finding out whether it has been finished in any special way, because the wrong treatment when laundering or cleaning could spoil the finish. Instructions are usually supplied to the shops by the manufacturers and are available to the public.

SHRINK-RESISTANCE

Fabrics made from cotton or wool are very inclined to shrink, but the shrinkage can now be controlled. Cottons that have been treated usually have one of the following marks—Sanforized, Anti-shrink, Non-shrink, Fully shrunk. Labels to look for on woollen fabrics are Dylan, Epilox and B.D.A.

CREASE-RESISTANCE

Cotton, Linen and Rayon fabrics all crease badly but a treatment that makes synthetic resins penetrate into the fibres makes them more resilient so that they either resist creasing or recover from it easily. Marks to look for are Tebilized, Carefree, Minicare and Minimum iron.

Glazed Finishes

The sheen on these cotton fabrics is produced either by Calendering, which is a kind of ironing using heated cylinders with the effect made durable by the application of synthetic resins, or by Schreinering, which is a method of embossing the fabric with fine diagonal lines which are also fixed with resins.

Mercerizing is a third method of giving cotton yarn and fabric an attractive gloss. The yarn or fabric is passed through a solution of caustic soda then stretched as it is being rinsed. The result is permanent.

Flame-resistance

Cotton, Linen and Rayon fabrics are all inflammable but they can all be treated chemically so that they will not flare up but only char. The name of the finish is Proban.

Raising or Brushing

This finish is used on Cotton, Rayon and Nylon to give them a warm and comfortable feeling. The fabric is passed between rollers, one of which is smooth and the other covered with short wires which raise the surface.

Embossing

This treatment gives the fabric a raised pattern which is achieved by passing the fabric between hot rollers and setting the result with synthetic resin.

Stiffening

Some fabrics are treated with resins and others have rayon threads woven in with the cotton threads and then the fabric is heat treated to melt the rayon. This method is known as Trubenizing.

Tutoring

Tutoring is done by weaving some groups of threads more tightly than others. This gives a puckered or crinkled appearance known as Seersucker. A similar effect is achieved after weaving by shrinking certain sections of the fabric, but this is less durable.

Moth-proofing

Untreated wool can be badly damaged by moth grubs, but damage can be prevented with a harmless chemical which the grubs dislike. Mitin, Dielmoth and Moth-proofed are labels to look for.

INTERFACINGS

An interfacing is a fabric attached to the wrong side of a garment or part of a garment such as collar, cuffs, lapels, to give extra firmness or permanent shape. It is also used as a backing for buttonholes and pockets to strengthen them.

Interfacing materials are made specially for their purpose and the variety of types, weights, and textures makes it possible to find one that is suitable for any kind of material. Sheer or transparent fabrics present most difficulty, but if strengthening is essential fine matching net or organdie can be used.

Interfacings can be divided into three main groups—

Woven Interfacings

These have warp and weft threads which makes it important that they must be cut on the same grain as the section of garment which is to be interfaced. This group includes the hair and linen canvases that tailors use, as well as cotton canvas and stiffened muslin and some fine lightweight cottons of varying degrees of stiffness which are adhesive. The last two will wash, but canvas shrinks when dampened therefore it can only be used on garments which will be dry cleaned. Stiffened muslins tend to lose their stiffness if washed.

Non-woven or Bonded Interfacings

These look rather like thin felt and have no grain; they are economical to use because the pattern pieces can be fitted on in any direction. They are obtainable in a number of different weights in white, black and grey. They will wash and dry-clean and do not stretch or fray.

Adhesive or Iron-on Interfacings

These are lightweight, both woven and bonded and have a special backing which fuses to the fabric when pressed with a hot iron. They give very pleasing results when used to interface collars and cuffs on cotton garments and they are more useful than any other type of interfacing for buttonholes and pockets as they prevent fraying, are not bulky, and need no sewing to keep them in place.

Good results are obtained when the lightest type of bonded adhesive interfacing is used on the collars, cuffs and pocket edges of jersey fabrics as it prevents stretching. Loosely-woven fabrics are easier to handle if backed with adhesive.

Be guided by the weight of your fabric and the degree of stiffness required when choosing an interfacing.

CARE OF FABRICS

Ready-made garments nearly always have either a sewn-in or a hanging label giving instructions for laundering and cleaning.

COTTON AND LINEN FABRICS

These are easy to launder and can be boiled, bleached and scrubbed without harm but they must be thoroughly rinsed. They need a hot iron, and better results are obtained if the fabric is damp; a steam iron is useful.

WOOLLEN FABRICS

These need special care, and all but the thinnest should be dry-cleaned.

When laundering jerseys a solution of warm water and detergent should be used. The garment must be totally immersed and gently squeezed, not rubbed, twisted or wrung. Soda should never be used. Rinse very thoroughly, spin dry, and press on the wrong side while still damp.

SILKS

Silk should always be washed gently in luke-warm water and detergent. Rinse several times, and for the last rinse use cold water. Dry by rolling in a cloth, iron while still damp with a warm iron on the wrong side. Wild silks must be ironed dry. Heavy silks, stiff silks and velvets should be dry-cleaned.

RAYONS

These can be washed in hand-hot water and detergent. Do not rub, twist or wring as the fibres are weak when wet. Rinse well, and dry by rolling in a towel. Press when slightly damp using a medium hot iron, (less hot for acetate rayon) on the wrong side. Tricel must be hand washed, cold rinsed and drip dried. Iron slightly damp using a steam iron. Knitted rayons rarely need ironing. All rayons can be dry-cleaned but they must be labelled.

NYLON

Garments made of nylon should be washed often using detergent; coloured nylon needs cooler water than white nylon. Rinse well and then drip dry away from direct heat or sun. Iron with a cool iron; jerseys do not need ironing.

TERYLENE

This can be washed by hand or machine in fairly hot water and detergent. Rinse well and drip-dry but do not spin. If ironing is needed use a warm iron or a steam iron.

ACRYLIC FABRICS

These should be washed gently in hand-hot water and detergent then rinsed three times, the last time using cold water. Roll in a towel and hang to dry. Press if necessary with a cool iron when completely dry. Do not use steam.

3
Taking Measurements

It is necessary to have accurate figure measurements before buying a pattern. Do not try to measure yourself; ask someone to help you and follow the instructions below. First remove belts and thick clothing.

Bust

Place the tape round the fullest part of the bust, raising the tape slightly at the back, and keeping two fingers inside the tape to prevent the measurement being taken too tightly (*see* Fig. 11).

Waist

Place tape round the natural waistline, firmly but not tightly. It should be possible to move the tape to the left and right easily (*see* Fig. 11).

Hips

Place the tape round the largest part of the hips, again with two fingers inside (*see* Fig. 11).

Nape to Waist

Measure from the most prominent bone in the nape of the neck, down the centre back to the waist (*see* Fig. 12).

Across Back

Measure between natural armhole lines, about 10 cm down from nape (*see* Fig. 12).

Full Length

Measure from nape to required length, holding tape close to waist (*see* Fig. 12).

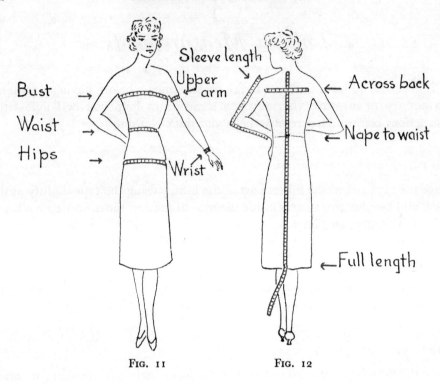

FIG. 11   FIG. 12

SLEEVE LENGTH

Place hand on hip and measure from bend of shoulder to the elbow and then to the wrist. Note both measurements (*see* Fig. 12).

UPPER ARM

Place tape round the largest part of the arm (*see* Fig. 11).

WRIST

Measure closely round wrist (*see* Fig. 11).

4

Choosing and Altering the Pattern

CHOOSING the pattern is the first step towards choosing a new garment, so there are several things that you must be sure of before you begin looking at the fashion books.

The occasions on which you will be wearing this garment are your first consideration. To be dressed suitably is one of the important rules for the well-dressed girl. Is the garment for casual wear or for more formal occasions? Having made your decision you will know in which section of the fashion book to look for your style.

Next you should know yourself. Study your figure and your posture, even your disposition (vivacious or quiet), and your favourite activities; these things should all influence you in your choice. Experiment in front of a full-length mirror; the right style can do a great deal to hide figure faults and to accentuate good points. Does a full, bunchy skirt really suit you? Does a high neckline flatter the shape of your face? If, for instance, you have a thick waist, you should choose unfitted styles that do not emphasize the waist. And if you have sloping shoulders, set-in sleeves will suit you better than raglan styles. Remember, too, that vertical lines have a slimming effect, and horizontal lines break up a tall thin figure. Never choose a style because you have admired it on someone else. Try to be individual in your style of dressing and you will soon build up a reputation for being well dressed.

The next step is to know your size. It is worth while waiting a day or two for the shop to get your correct size if it is out of stock. Buy dress, blouse, suit, jacket, housecoat and underwear patterns by your bust size. Buy skirt, shorts, slacks patterns by your waist size.

Choose a pattern supplied by one of the well-known pattern makers, because their instructions for making the garment are much easier to follow, and be content with simple styles until you have gained some experience.

Your pattern envelope will show two or three variations of the chosen style; these are either numbered or lettered and are referred to as "views." Decide which view you intend to make and turn to the back of the envelope to find out what fabrics are recommended and the amount needed. The latter will vary according to the size of the pattern and the view chosen, so check carefully. A list of the accessories needed to make up the garment is also given (threads, fastenings, lace, etc.) and these should be bought when you buy the material.

ALTERATIONS

Commercial patterns are made to standardized measurements, but a large number of people find that their personal measurements are not standard, and the patterns need a little alteration to make them fit perfectly. The position of the alteration is governed by the style of the garment, and care must be taken not to interfere with the style. Most patterns indicate where the pattern pieces should be shortened or lengthened. Alteration of one piece of pattern usually necessitates the alteration of other pieces in order that the pieces should fit together. If the neck is changed in either the size or shape, the collar or facing will have to be altered; likewise, any alteration to the armhole will mean that the sleevehead must be altered too.

To Shorten the Bodice

Make a tuck half the depth of the required alteration, across both back and front pattern pieces, at right angles to the straight grain line, and about half

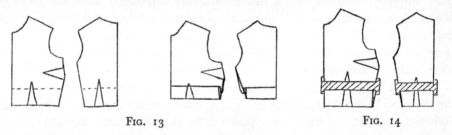

Fig. 13   Fig. 14

way between the armhole and the bottom edge. The cutting and fitting lines of the side seam will need to be straightened (*see* Fig. 13).

To Lengthen the Bodice

Draw a line across both the back and front pieces of pattern, about half way between the armhole and the bottom edge. Cut across on line, separate the two sections by the required amount and insert a strip of paper. The side seam may need slight adjustment (*see* Fig. 14).

To Shorten a Long Sleeve

Make a tuck across the width of the sleeve, either between the elbow and the underarm or between the elbow and the wrist. If the alteration is to be more than 2·5 cms, the sleeve shape is kept more easily by making a small tuck in both positions. Adjust fitting lines (*see* Fig. 15).

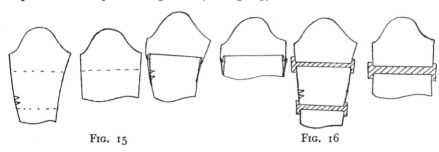

Fig. 15　　　　　　　　Fig. 16

To Lengthen a Long Sleeve

Slash sleeve across in same positions as above and insert strips of paper of required depth (*see* Fig. 16).

To Shorten the Skirt

Make a tuck just below the hip line and if necessary make another about half way between that and the hem (*see* Fig. 17).

Fig. 17　　　　　　　　Fig. 18

To Lengthen the Skirt

Slash skirt across in same positions as above and insert strips of paper: remember to adjust seam line in both cases (*see* Fig. 18).

To Make Waistline Smaller

Divide the required amount of alteration between all waist darts and increase each dart by that amount. If the alteration is fairly large, then substitute each dart for two smaller ones. Two small darts give better shaping than one large one (*see* Fig. 19).

To Make the Pattern Pieces Narrower

Often this particular alteration is needed only on the bodice back. Make a vertical tuck of the required width from the shoulder to the waist, running parallel with the straight grain; straighten the shoulder fitting line. Make a

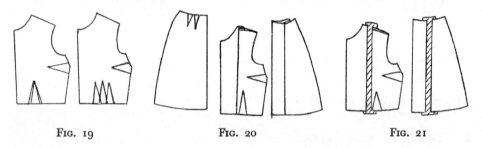

FIG. 19　　　　　FIG. 20　　　　　FIG. 21

small dart in the front shoulder so that the F. and B. shoulders will fit together. If the garment is a dress, make a similar tuck in the back skirt pattern or make an extra dart in the skirt waist, to ensure that the bodice and skirt will fit together (*see* Fig. 20).

To Make the Pattern Pieces Wider

Back widths vary considerably from person to person, and therefore this alteration may be needed only on the bodice back. Cut the pattern vertically from shoulder to waist and insert a strip of paper of the required width. Make a small dart in the back shoulder or add the required amount to the armhole edge of the front shoulder, so that B. and F. shoulders will fit together (*see* Fig. 21).

A person with a large bust may need to widen the bodice front only. Cut the front bodice pattern vertically from shoulder to waist and insert a strip of paper of the required width. Reduce the front shoulder to fit the back shoulder by means of a dart. Make an extra dart in the front waist so that it will fit the skirt.

The skirt may be widened in a similar manner for persons with large hips, but remember to make extra darts in the waist if the bodice has not been altered.

5
Using the Pattern

PREPARATION OF THE PATTERN

1. Identify the pattern pieces (they are all either numbered or lettered).
2. Put away all sections not required.
3. Note the meaning of all pattern markings (these will be given on your instruction sheet).
4. Check the length of the pattern pieces with your own measurements and alter if necessary.
5. Pin pattern together and try it on; this will show you whether the style lines are in the right places, and the darts the right length (*see* Fig. 22).

FIG. 22

Fitting the pattern

6. Remove pattern, correct if necessary and smooth out in readiness for use.

PREPARATION OF THE MATERIAL

1. Iron all creases from material.
2. Note faults and mark them, so that they can be avoided when laying on the pattern.
3. Check the grain; when the material is folded with the selvedges together the torn edge should lie flat and even. If it will not do so, pull the material diagonally throughout its length until it lies flat (*see* Fig. 23).
4. Note whether the material has a nap or pile or "one-way" design. Materials with a pile surface (velvet) look lighter when hung with the pile

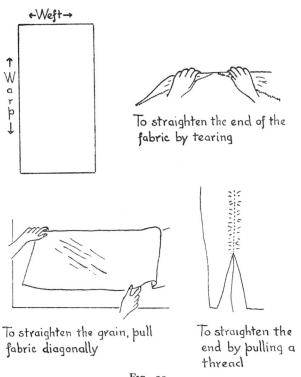

←Weft→

↑ Warp ↓

To straighten the end of the fabric by tearing

To straighten the grain, pull fabric diagonally

To straighten the end by pulling a thread

FIG. 23

lying downwards than they do when the pile runs upwards. When laying the pattern on the material it is therefore necessary that care should be taken to see that the pile lies in the same direction on each pattern piece. The same rule applies to materials printed with a design that looks different when hung the reverse way.

LAYING ON THE PATTERN

1. Choose the lay given for your size and width of material.
2. Fold the material as instructed and lay the pattern on as shown.
3. Make sure that fold marks are put to a fold in the material.
4. Check straight grain marks by measuring from the selvedge to each end of the mark.
5. Pin firmly inside the cutting line, using extra pins round curves.
6. Lay all pattern pieces on the material before cutting, unless the material has to be refolded.

CUTTING OUT

1. Use sharp scissors with blades at least 15 cms long.
2. Put your left hand firmly on the pattern and cut with the whole length of the scissors blades along the cutting line, pushing the lower blade along the table. Keep the material flat on the table the whole time.
3. Cut notches outwards, not into the seam allowance.
4. Do not remove the pattern.

MARKING OUT

All pattern marks, except straight grain marks, must be transferred to the material before removing the pattern.
There are three methods—
1. Tailor's chalk can be used, but since it rubs off easily, it should be used only for temporary marking. It is not very accurate, particularly on materials that have a fluffy surface.

2. A tracing-wheel and carbon paper can be used with greater accuracy, but care must be taken that the marks are transferred to the W.S. of the material, because it may not be possible to remove the marks from some materials (*see* Fig. 24).

3. Thread-marking is the most satisfactory method to use because, if done correctly, it is both accurate and lasting (*see* Fig. 25).

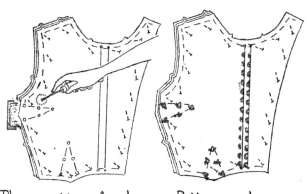

Place one piece of carbon paper between the pattern and the material, and a second piece underneath both layers of material

FIG. 24

Pattern marks transferred by means of tailor tacks

FIG. 25

METHOD FOR THREAD-MARKING

1. Mark all folds with a single line of straight tacking. *Tailor tacking* is used whenever marking has to be done on double material. Using double cotton, make a small stitch in the required place through both layers of material, leaving an end of about 2 cms. Make a second stitch in the same place, leaving a loop. Cut the thread, leaving another end (*see* Fig. 26). If a straight line, such as the fold line on the front of a blouse, has to be marked on double material, work a line of tacking, using double thread and leaving a loop between each stitch (*see* Fig. 27).

2. When the marking is completed, remove the pattern and carefully pull

the two layers of material apart, beginning at the edge and cutting the threads as you come to them. This will leave identical tufts of thread on both layers of material (*see* Figs. 28 and 29).

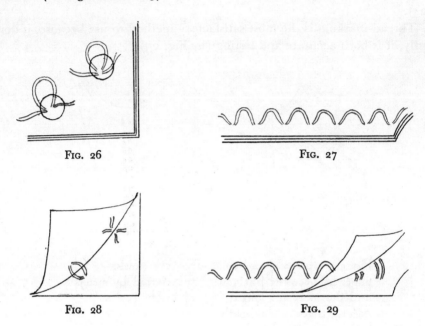

FIG. 26

FIG. 27

FIG. 28

FIG. 29

3. Use two or three different coloured cottons to help in identifying the pattern markings. This is particularly important when marking pleats.

6
Pressing

THE importance of pressing when making a garment cannot be stressed too strongly. Every stage of each process must be pressed before you go on to the next, if a professional finish is to be obtained. Pressing is not ironing. The iron must be lifted and pressed down again in a fresh place and never pushed along. Before pressing the garment, test the material for its reaction to heat and moisture on a scrap or corner. Remove tacking and pins before pressing. Make sure that the section to be pressed is lying quite flat and that no other part of the garment is being creased.

PRESSING OF VARIOUS PARTS OF THE GARMENT

Use the correct equipment, e.g. a skirt board for skirts (*see* Fig. 30), a sleeve board for sleeve seams and cuffs (*see* Fig. 31), a padded roller for seams, a

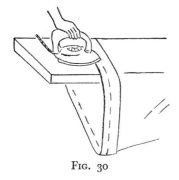

FIG. 30

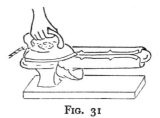

FIG. 31

tailor's cushion for darts, sleeve heads, and curves that are awkward to press on a flat surface.

SEAMS

Open a flat seam with the point of the iron; then, pulling the two sides well apart, press until the seam is flat on both R. and W. sides. The use of a padded

43

roller will prevent the edges of the turnings from marking the material and from showing through on the R. S. French seams should first of all be pressed to flatten the machining and then to one side, usually the back, making sure that

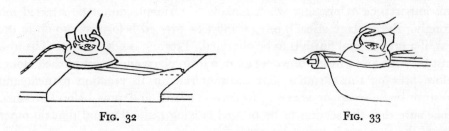

FIG. 32   FIG. 33

the R.S. is perfectly flat. More details on this and other seams are given in the chapter on Seams (*see* Figs. 32 and 33).

DARTS

Place the R.S. down on a tailor's cushion, pulling the sides well apart until there is no possibility of a groove or pleat forming on the R.S. Press first with the point of the iron along the stitch line, then press the dart to one side, making sure that the point of the dart is smooth and unwrinkled. If the dart has been

FIG. 34

slit, use the same method as for a plain seam, still using the tailor's cushion (*see* Fig. 34).

Waist darts and neck and shoulder darts should be pressed towards the centre. Other darts should be pressed so that the wide end lies evenly along the cut edge.

PLEATS

Each fold should be pressed separately on the underside; then, when the pleats are tacked into position, arrange on a completely flat surface and press on the W.S. Remove the tacks for final pressing.

ARMHOLE SEAM

Always press this seam towards the sleeve. Holding the tailor's cushion against your body, hang the sleeve head over it and press the seam lightly; then move to a fresh place. This can be done on the R.S., but a cloth should be used between the garment and the iron (*see* Fig. 35).

FIG. 35

PRESSING VARIOUS FABRICS

Cotton	Use a hot iron, and steam if necessary; cotton is usually pressed on the R.S.
Linen	Press slightly damp, using a hot iron and steam on the R.S.
Silk	A moderate iron should be used on the W.S. Steam may leave a water-mark.
Wool	A moderately hot iron should be used on the W.S. It scorches easily, therefore a pressing cloth must be used. Steam is essential, particularly on thick woollens. Wool fabrics must be tested for shrinkage before cutting out. Test by pressing a corner of the material under a damp cloth until dry. If the fabric is not shrink-resistant the whole of the fabric must be pressed under a damp cloth before it is used.

Rayon	Press on the W.S., using a cool iron and no steam.
Tricel	Use a moderate iron on the W.S.; steam can be helpful.
Nylon	Press lightly with a cool iron. No steam.
Terylene	Light pressing with a cool iron. No steam.
Fibrolane blend	Use the heat required for the other fibre in the blend.
Acrilan	Use a cool iron but no steam.
Courtelle	Use a cool iron but no steam.

7
Control of Fullness

A CERTAIN amount of fullness is necessary in all garments in order that they may be comfortable to wear, but this fullness must be controlled and it is the method of control that helps to give the garment its shape and style.

DARTS

This is an inconspicuous method of control and is used wherever a smooth, fitted effect is desired.

The most usual positions for darts are the waist of both bodice and skirt; the bust or underarm; the shoulder; the back neck; the elbow (*see* Figs. 36, 37, 38, 39). A dart is wedge-shaped, with the widest part at the edge of the material.

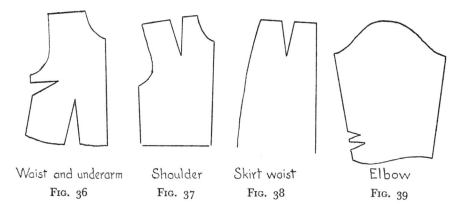

Waist and underarm	Shoulder	Skirt waist	Elbow
FIG. 36	FIG. 37	FIG. 38	FIG. 39

METHOD OF WORKING A DART

1. Transfer marks from pattern to material accurately (*see* Fig. 40).

2. Fold the material R.S. together, with the two marks nearest the edge on top of one another and the fold extending to the single mark at the end of the dart (*see* Fig. 41).

3. Pin and tack in a straight line from the wide end, tapering off to nothing at the point.

4. Machine from the wide end towards the point, bringing the stitching right off the fold at the end. Tie off the ends (*see* Fig. 42).

5. Press the dart to one side (*see* Fig. 43).

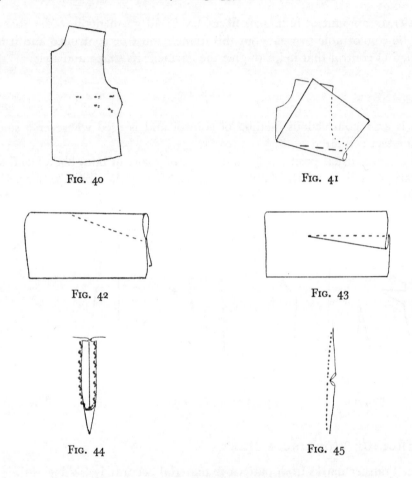

FIG. 40   FIG. 41

FIG. 42   FIG. 43

FIG. 44   FIG. 45

If very thick material is used, the dart may be slit along the fold to within 3 cms of the point and pressed open (*see* Fig. 44).

Darts pointed at both ends are used on a garment with no waist seam, and are machined from point to point. They must be snipped at the centre to make them lie flat; the snip is neatened with blanket stitching (*see* Fig. 45).

DART TUCKS

These are worked in the same way as darts, but the machining stops short before reaching the point. The finished dart tuck has the appearance of a small pleat on the R.S. (*see* Figs. 46, 47, 48).

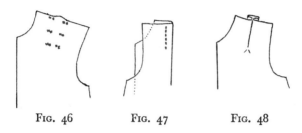

FIG. 46   FIG. 47   FIG. 48

GATHERING

This has a decorative and soft effect and is used at the shoulder and waist of bodices, at skirt waists and at sleeve ends. Soft, fine material is most suitable.

METHOD OF GATHERING

1. Begin on the fitting line, with the thread secured firmly, and continue with tiny running stitches for the required length; leave the end hanging (*see* Fig. 49).

2. Work a second line, 0·5 cm outside the fitting line (this helps to control the gathers and makes them easier to handle (*see* Fig. 50).

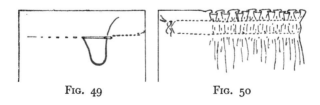

FIG. 49   FIG. 50

3. Pull both threads together until drawn up to the required size, wind the ends round a pin and distribute the gathers evenly.

EASING

This is gathering where there is very little fullness, such as a sleeve head. The method is the same.

SHIRRING

This describes several rows of gathering evenly spaced. It is decorative, and is often used on children's clothes.

PLEATS

A pleat is made by folding the material until you have three thicknesses. They are secured at one end only and can be pressed or left unpressed, according to the style and material being used. A firm, closely woven fabric is more suitable for a pleated style than a soft material. The pleats may be left to hang free or they may be stitched part of the way down. They are smart and decorative and allow for easy movement.

A knife pleat consists of one single pleat (*see* Fig. 51).

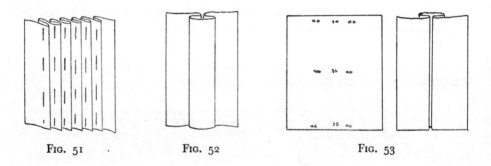

FIG. 51   FIG. 52   FIG. 53

A box pleat is made of two knife pleats turned away from one another on the R.S. (*see* Fig. 52).

An inverted pleat is made of two knife pleats turned towards one another on the R.S. (*see* Fig. 53).

METHOD FOR UNPRESSED PLEATS

1. The fold lines should be clearly marked on the material in two colours (*see* Fig. 54).

2. Follow your pattern instructions for the direction of the pleats, and bring one mark over to the next one of a different colour.

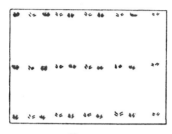

FIG. 54

3. Put a pin through the three thicknesses of material.

4. Continue until all the pleats are in position, then tack firmly and remove the pins.

METHOD FOR PRESSED PLEATS

1. Work on a flat surface where the whole length of the pleat can lie flat.

2. Working on the R.S. of the material, pin and tack and press each fold from top to bottom.

3. Place fold to indicated mark and secure with diagonal tacking through three layers of material.

4. Press thoroughly on the W.S.

AN INVERTED PLEAT USING A PLEAT BACKING

1. Tack and press the folds on the two sections.

2. Mark the centre of the backing strip.

3. Place the folds so that they meet on the centre mark of the backing strip.

4. Tack into position and turn to W.S.

5. Pin, tack and machine the raw edges together (*see* Fig. 55).
6. Machine the pleats for part of their length on the R.S. (*see* Fig. 56).

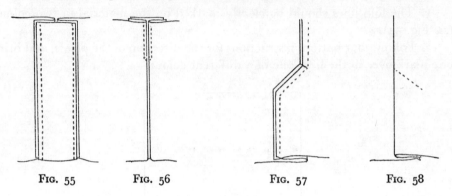

FIG. 55   FIG. 56   FIG. 57   FIG. 58

KNIFE PLEAT IN CENTRE-BACK SEAM

1. Pin, tack and machine C.B. seam, following pleat line (*see* Fig. 57).
2. Snip into corner and press seam open above pleat.
3. Let fold of pleat fall into place naturally, tack and press.
4. Strengthen by machining across top of pleat (*see* Fig. 58).

TUCKS

A tuck is a fold of material stitched through the double fabric on the R.S. They can be any size from 2 mm (pin-tucks) upwards. They can be used as a purely decorative feature (*see* Fig. 59), or to control fullness in place of darts or gathering. They are also used on children's clothes to allow for growth.

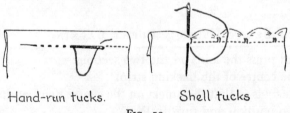

Hand-run tucks.   Shell tucks

FIG. 59

Tucks other than pin-tucks are marked on patterns by solid and broken lines or by two sizes of perforations. If pin-tucking is to be used for collars or cuffs or for complete panels, it is better to tuck a piece of material and place the pattern on it afterwards.

METHOD FOR TUCKS

1. Make a tuck marker from thin card. This should show the required width of the tuck and the space between (*see* Fig. 60).

2. Working on the R.S. of the material, press the first fold along its whole length.

3. Measure width of tuck from fold with marker and tack through two layers of material (*see* Fig. 61).

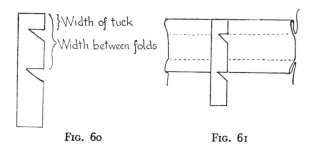

FIG. 60   FIG. 61

4. Machine on side that is to be uppermost.
5. Press into position.
6. Using marker, find the position of the second tuck fold, and press.
7. Proceed as for first tuck.

8
Seams

A SEAM is a method of fixing together two pieces of material and can be conspicuous or inconspicuous according to the method used. The type of seam chosen must be the one best suited to the fabric and to its place on the garment. It must be strong, neat, well stitched and pressed.

Inconspicuous seams can be plain or open seams or French seams.

Conspicuous seams are overlaid or lapped seams or double-stitched seams.

THE PLAIN OR OPEN SEAM

This seam is very flat and is used on a wide variety of garments and materials, the exception being transparent materials.

METHOD

1. Place two pieces of material, R.S. together, with notches and fitting lines matching.
2. Pin, tack and machine on the fitting line (*see* Fig. 62).

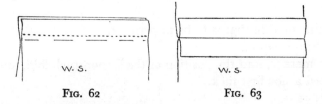

FIG. 62   FIG. 63

3. Tie off ends and remove tacks.
4. Press seam open (*see* Fig. 63).

NEATENING

The method of neatening depends on the type of material used.

1. For cottons, thin silks and rayons, turn the raw edges under and machine close to the fold (*see* Fig. 64).

2. For firmly woven woollens and heavy silks, the raw edges should be over-cast or blanket-stitched finely (*see* Figs. 65 and 66).

3. For loosely woven materials, which fray badly, the edges should be bound with Paris or bias binding (*see* Fig. 67).

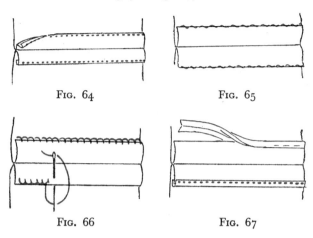

FIG. 64   FIG. 65

FIG. 66   FIG. 67

THE FRENCH SEAM

This seam is self-neatening and is used on thin materials and garments that require washing.

METHOD

1. Place two pieces of material W.S. together, with notches and fitting lines matching.

2. Pin and tack on the fitting line (*see* Fig. 68).

3. Machine the finished width of the seam outside the fitting line. (This may vary according to the material used. Average 0·5 cm.) (*See* Fig. 69.)

4. Trim turnings to less than the finished width of the seam and press open. (This makes the next step easier.) (*See* Fig. 69.)

5. Turn so that the R.S. of the material is inside and crease along the line of stitching. Pin, tack and machine on the fitting line (*see* Fig. 70).

6. Remove tacks and press the seam to one side (*see* Fig. 71).

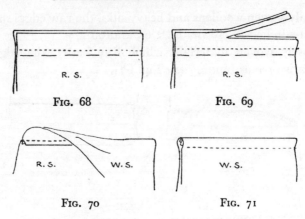

FIG. 68   FIG. 69

FIG. 70   FIG. 71

THE OVERLAID OR LAPPED SEAM

This is a decorative seam, which emphasizes the seam line with machine stitching on the R.S. It is used on yokes, panels and frills and most materials are suitable except transparent ones.

METHOD

1. The fitting line must be marked on both the sections to be joined (*see* Fig. 72).

2. Turn the seam allowance on the upper section to the W.S. and press (*see* Fig. 73).

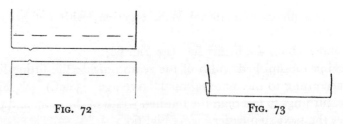

FIG. 72   FIG. 73

3. Place the fold exactly on the fitting line of the lower section. Pin and tack. (If the lower section is a frill, the fold is placed on the gathering line on the fitting line.)

4. Machine close to the fold or an even distance from it, providing the machining holds the three layers of material (*see* Fig. 74).

5. Press and neaten by oversewing or blanket-stitching both turnings together (*see* Fig. 75).

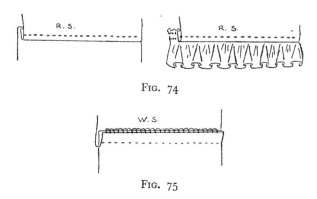

FIG. 74

FIG. 75

THE DOUBLE-STITCHED SEAM

This is a strong seam, which can be worked on either side of the material. Worked on the W.S., and showing only one row of machining on the R.S., it is used for winter pyjamas and housecoats of patterned material. Worked on the R.S., and showing two rows of machining on the R.S., it is used for shirt-blouses, overalls, unlined jackets, blazers and dressing-gowns. The same seam worked by hand is called the run-and-fell seam and is used on baby-clothes, because it is soft and flat. This seam is also self-neatening.

METHOD (worked on W.S.)

1. Place two pieces of material, R.S. together, and pin, tack and machine on the fitting line. Remove tacks (*see* Fig. 76).

2. Trim the back turning to half its width. Press the seam open and then press the front turning over the back turning.

3. Turn the raw edge of the front turning under to meet the back turning, then pin and tack to garment (*see* Fig. 77).

4. Machine close to fold and press (*see* Fig. 78).

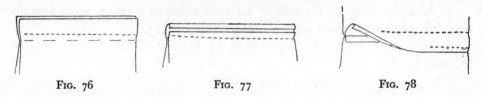

FIG. 76   FIG. 77   FIG. 78

METHOD (worked on R.S.)

1. Place two pieces of material, W.S. together; pin, tack and machine on the fitting line, then proceed as above.

THE CURVED SEAM

If a seam is curved, the turnings must be either snipped or notched, to make them lie flat. If the turnings curl up when being pressed, they must be snipped, so that the edges can stretch and lie against the garment (*see* Fig. 79). If the

FIG. 79   FIG. 80

edges of the turnings wrinkle or pleat when being pressed, they must be notched to get rid of the surplus material (*see* Fig. 80).

THE WAIST SEAM

When joining the bodice to the skirt, place them, R.S. together, with centres, side seams and notches matching. Pin, tack and machine on the fitting line and press the seam towards the bodice. The turnings should be neatened together with Paris or bias binding.

CROSSED SEAMS

When it is necessary for two seams to cross one another, the first seam must be neatened and pressed before working the second seam (*see* Fig. 81). When

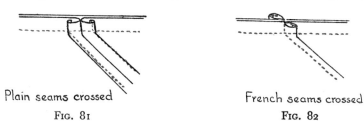

Plain seams crossed
Fig. 81

French seams crossed
Fig. 82

crossing French seams, press the fells of the two seams to be joined in opposite directions and then match the two fitting lines (*see* Fig. 82).

THE ANGLED SEAM

If a seam has to be worked round a corner, the best and most suitable seam to use is the lapped seam (Figs. 84 and 85), but if this is not possible and a plain

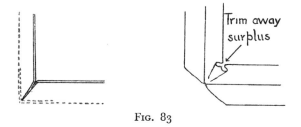

Trim away
surplus

Fig. 83

seam has to be used, the corner must be strengthened either with extra lines of machining or by using small patches on the W.S. to prevent the material tearing under strain. Fig. 83 shows the angle strengthened by extra machining and Figs. 86–88 show the working of the angled underarm seam of a dolman or kimono sleeve strengthened by patches.

FIGS. 84 and 85. Lapped Seam Used on a Corner.

THE ANGLED UNDERARM SEAM FOR A DOLMAN SLEEVE

1. Cut four squares of material, 6 cms by 6 cms, and press 0·5 cm turnings to the W.S. on all sides (*see* Fig. 86).

2. Place one square on the W.S. of each section of the garment and machine close to the fold. Cut to fit the edge of the garment. (*See* Fig. 87).

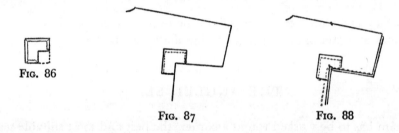

FIG. 86   FIG. 87   FIG. 88

3. Place B. and F. sections of the garment R.S. together, and pin, tack and machine on the fitting line (*see* Fig. 88).

4. Snip into the corner, press the seam open and neaten.

9
Crossway Strips

Crossway strips have many uses—
1. Neatening edges (binding and facing).
2. Fabric loops (rouleau).
3. Piping.
4. Attaching collars and cuffs.

Crossway strips are used for these purposes because they are elastic and can be eased or stretched round curved edges and still remain smooth and flat.

Method of Cutting Crossway Strips

1. Fold the material so that the warp threads lie parallel with the weft threads (*see* Fig. 89).
2. Press the resulting fold.

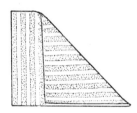 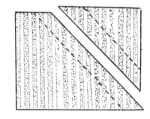

Fig. 89 Fig. 90

3. Open the material out flat and cut along the crease.
4. Measure from the cut edge the width required and mark with pencil dots.
5. Cut along the marked line (*see* Fig. 90).

Method of Joining Crossway Strips

1. Always join on the straight grain.
2. Cut the ends of the strips to be joined along a thread, so that the edges, and pattern, if any, match.
3. Place the strips, R.S. together, and lying at right-angles to one another. Pin and tack (*see* Fig. 91).

4. Machine 0·5 cm from the edges.
5. Open the seam and press flat (*see* Fig. 92).
6. Trim off protruding points.

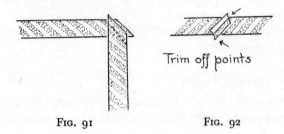

FIG. 91   FIG. 92

BINDING WITH A CROSSWAY STRIP

This is a decorative way of neatening an edge and is visible on both sides of the garment. A self-coloured or contrasting strip can be used. The strip should be cut four times the finished width of the binding, the average width being 0·5 cm.

METHOD

1. Trim the turnings on the edge to be bound to 0·5 cm.
2. With the R.S. of the strip to the R.S. of the garment, pin and tack 0·5 cm from the edge.
3. Machine on tacking line (*see* Fig. 93).

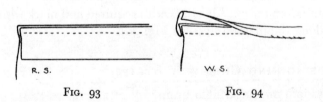

FIG. 93   FIG. 94

4. Fold the free edge of the strip to meet the edge of the garment.
5. Bring the fold over to the stitch line, pin, and hem to the machine stitches. Press (*see* Fig. 94).

Stretch the strip slightly when binding round corners and concave curves, such as necklines. Ease the strip slightly when binding round convex curves, such as scallops (*see* Figs. 95, 96, 97).

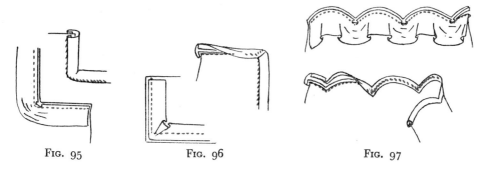

FIG. 95   FIG. 96   FIG. 97

PIPING

Piping can be done either with or without a cord and is a decorative method of accentuating the style-lines of yokes and the edges of collars. It is also used on soft furnishings, as a finish to the seams of cushion covers and loose covers.

METHOD 1—PIPING WITHOUT CORD

1. Using a warm iron, stretch the crossway strip slightly and fold it in half lengthways.

2. Place the stretched and folded crossway strip between the seam edges

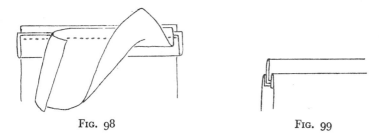

FIG. 98   FIG. 99

with the fold extending beyond the fitting line towards the garment. Tack and machine on the fitting line (*see* Fig. 98).

3. Turn seam R.S. out and press (*see* Fig. 99).

METHOD 2—USING A LAPPED SEAM

1. Prepare the crossway strip as for first method.

2. Turn under the seam allowance on the top section. Pin and tack to folded crossway strip, 0·25–0·5 cm from the fold (*see* Fig. 100).

3. Place fitting line of top section over fitting line of under section. Pin, tack and machine on the fitting line. Press (*see* Fig. 101).

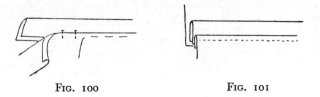

FIG. 100   FIG. 101

PIPING WITH CORD

1. Shrink cord before using it.

2. Stretch the crossway strip, fold it round the cord and secure it with running stitches close to the cord (*see* Fig. 102).

3. Place the covered cord between the seam edges, with the cord extending just beyond the fitting line. Tack.

4. Machine, using a cording or zipper foot on the machine (*see* Fig. 103).

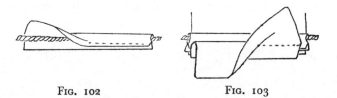

FIG. 102   FIG. 103

10

Openings

ALL garments that fit fairly closely need openings of some sort. Whatever their position, openings are used and handled a great deal and are often subjected to strain. Openings must be strongly made and extra care must be taken to strengthen the closed ends. The type of opening is chosen according to its position and to the kind of material used.

Openings can be conspicuous and related to the style of the garment, or concealed, but whichever they are, the working must be careful, accurate and neatly finished, with both sides exactly the same length. They must be long enough for the garment to be put on and removed easily. The average lengths are—

Side of skirt	.	.	.	. 20 cms
Side of dress	.	.	.	. 30 cms
Back of dress	.	.	.	. 50 cms
Wrist .	.	.	.	. 8 cms

For people bigger than average the opening should be longer.

BODICE-FRONT OPENING

This is a simple opening, consisting only of the facings turned to the W.S. on the fold lines of the L. and R. fronts respectively and then lapped over one another with the centre fronts matching (*see* Figs. 104, 105, 106).

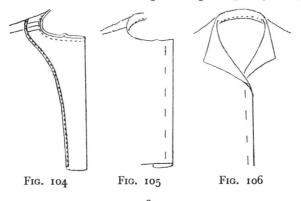

FIG. 104   FIG. 105   FIG. 106

CONTINUOUS-STRIP OPENINGS

This opening is inconspicuous, hard wearing, and popular and is used on sleeves, panties, pyjamas and waist slips. It can be worked in a slit or a seam (*see* Figs. 107 and 108).

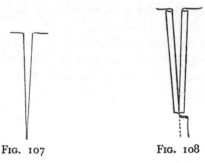

FIG. 107   FIG. 108

METHOD IN A SLIT

1. Cut a strip on the straight grain, twice the length of the opening by twice the finished width of the strip, plus 0·5 cm turnings.

2. Open the slit out straight and place the R.S. of the strip to the R.S. of the opening. Pin 0·5 cm turnings to within 2 cm of the end of the slit, then pull the end of the slit down until it is almost 0·5 cm below the edge of the strip. Treat the other side of the opening in the same way (*see* Fig. 109).

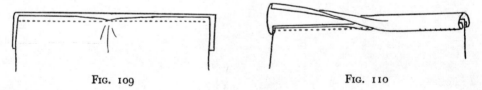

FIG. 109   FIG. 110

3. Tack and machine from garment side 0·5 cm from the edge. Stop machining with the needle down in the work at the base of the slit; raise the foot and move the fold to the rear of the needle; continue machining.

4. Press the turnings towards the strip and press a 0·5 cm turning on the free edge of the strip.

5. Fold the strip over to the W.S. of the opening. Tack and hem to the machine stitching (*see* Fig. 110).

6. Press the strip back on the top side of the opening and let the under side project (*see* Fig. 111).

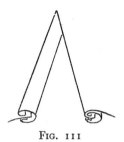

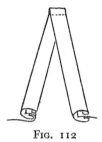

FIG. 111   FIG. 112

7. Backstitch across the fold at the end of the opening to strengthen (*see* Fig. 112).

METHOD IN SEAM

    1. Complete the seam to the base of the opening.
    2. Cut across the turnings at this point and blanket-stitch.
    3. Trim the turnings on the opening to 0·5 cm (*see* Fig. 108).
    4. Continue as for the method in the slit.

BOUND OPENING

This is a less bulky method than the previous one, though not quite as strong. It is suitable for use on transparent material. It is frequently used on the front opening of the skirt of a shirt-waister dress, where it is hidden by a pleat.

    1. Mark the opening with tacking or chalk and machine 3 mm away from the mark, down one side and up the other, taking one stitch across the base (*see* Fig. 113).

    2. Cut between the machining to the base (*see* Fig. 114).

    3. Cut a crossway strip, twice the length of the opening and four times the finished width of the bind.

4. Place R.S. of binding to R.S. of opening; pin, tack and machine 0·5 cm from the edge; roll binding over to W.S. and hem to machine stitching. Press (*see* Figs. 115 and 116).

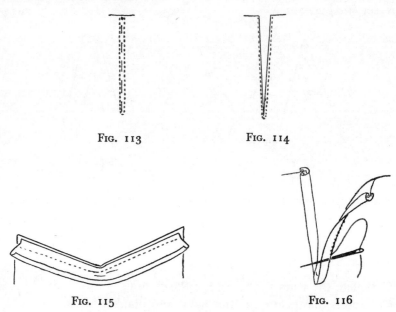

FIG. 113   FIG. 114

FIG. 115   FIG. 116

FACED-SLIT OPENING

This opening can be used on most light-weight materials, with the exception of transparent ones. It is used as a sleeve opening, particularly if the cuff is to be fastened with links, and as a neck opening on children's clothes. It is flat and neat but has no under- or overlap.

1. Mark the opening with a line of tacking (*see* Fig. 117).

2. Cut a piece of material on the straight grain, 7 cms wide and 4 cms longer than the opening.

3. Neaten by turning 0·5 cm to the W.S. on two long sides and one short side. Machine close to the fold and press.

4. Place R.S. of facing to R.S. of opening, with centre of facing on marked opening. Tack firmly into place (*see* Fig. 118).

5. Machine 3 mm from mark down one side and up the other, tapering slightly at the base and taking one stitch across the base (*see* Fig. 118).

6. Cut through both layers of material between the machining to within one thread of the machining at the base (*see* Fig. 119).

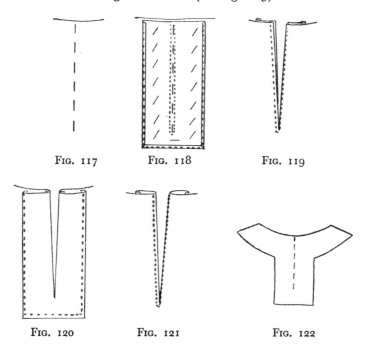

FIG. 117   FIG. 118   FIG. 119

FIG. 120   FIG. 121   FIG. 122

7. Turn the facing through to the W.S. and tack the seam at the edge (*see* Fig. 120). Press.

8. Machine round the edge of the opening on the R.S. to strengthen (*see* Fig. 121).

Neck facing and slit facing are often combined to avoid unnecessary seams (*see* Fig. 122).

PLACKETS

This is a flat and inconspicuous type of opening and is particularly useful on thick materials. It is used chiefly on woollen skirts and dresses. It can be neated with Paris binding or lining.

Skirt Placket Neatened with Paris Binding

1. Finish and neaten the seam up to the base of the opening and mark the fitting lines clearly on both sides of the opening (*see* Fig. 123).

2. Snip the back turning 1 cm below the base of the opening, so that it can form the underlap (*see* Fig. 123).

3. Cut four pieces of Paris binding, each 1 cm longer than the opening.

4. Catch-stitch one piece of binding to the W.S. of the front of the opening along the fitting line (*see* Fig. 124).

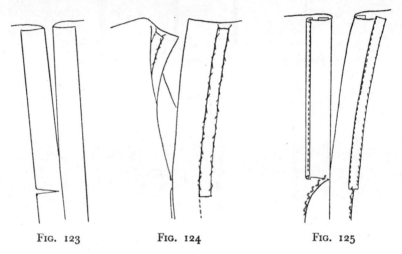

FIG. 123   FIG. 124   FIG. 125

5. Machine a second piece outside the fitting line on the W.S. of the back of the opening; the fastenings will be sewn through these two pieces (*see* Fig. 124).

6. Neaten the edge of the front turning by machining a strip of binding to the R.S. of the edge. Press the turning into position and catch-stitch the binding to the skirt (*see* Fig. 125).

7. Neaten the edge of the back turning by binding the edge with another strip of binding (*see* Fig. 125).

8. Lap the front over the back, with fitting lines together, and neaten the base with a short piece of binding (*see* Fig. 126).

9. Press and strengthen with a bar tack (*see* Fig. 127).

BAR TACK

Working on the R.S., make three or four stitches across the seam at the base of the opening. The stitches should be quite small. Work over these stitches to form a tiny bar. If matching cotton is used the bar tack will be almost invisible (*see* Fig. 128).

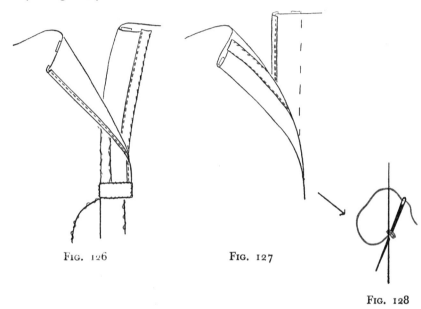

FIG. 126   FIG. 127

FIG. 128

DRESS PLACKET, USING LINING

1. The waist seam must be completed and pressed open at the ends (*see* Fig. 129).

2. Snip the back turning of the opening 1 cm beyond each end (*see* Fig. 129).

3. Cut two crossway strips of lining, 3 cms wide and 2 cms longer than the opening.

4. Pin, tack and machine one strip to the fitting-line on the R.S., to each side of the opening, as if it were a binding (*see* Figs. 130 and 131).

5. Turn under the free edge of the strip on the back opening, pin to machine-line and hem. This forms the underlap (*see* Fig. 131).

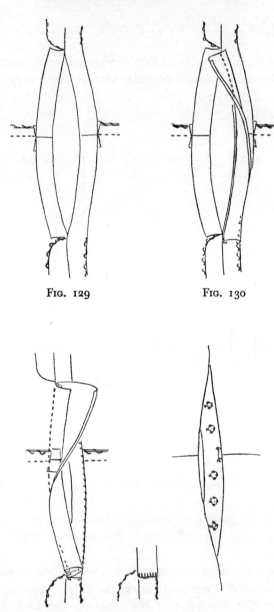

FIG. 129   FIG. 130

FIG. 131   FIG. 132   FIG. 133

6. Press front turning back on the fitting line; turn under free edge of strip; pin and hem to garment (*see* Fig. 130).

7. Place front fitting-line over back fitting-line; neaten both ends of the strips with blanket-stitching. Press (*see* Fig. 132).

8. Work bar at both ends of the opening.

9. Sew on fastenings, using a hook and bar at the waist (*see* Fig. 133).

THE ZIPPED OPENING

The zip fastener is both an opening and a fastening. It is neat and quick to use and is made in weights and colours to suit most materials. A zipped opening should be long enough to allow the garment to be removed easily, because strain on the closed end of the zip can ruin it.

There are three methods of inserting a zip fastener—

1. *Inserted in a slit.* The zip is visible and this method is used for short neck-openings, where there is no seam, and on pockets.

2. *Edge-to-edge or semi-concealed.* The zip is inserted in the C.B. seam of dresses and skirts.

3. *Concealed.* This method is used in the side seams of skirts.

Inserted in a Slit

1. Mark the length of the opening, measuring from the fitting-line.

2. Mark 0·5 cm turnings on both sides of the opening.

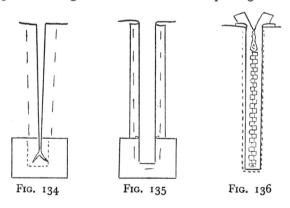

FIG. 134   FIG. 135   FIG. 136

3. Cut a small square of self material or lining, 3 cms by 3 cms, and place as shown in Fig. 134 on the R.S. of the material. Machine on marked line round the end of the opening.

4. Cut the opening to within 0·5 cm of the base and snip diagonally into the corners (*see* Fig. 134).

5. Turn lining through the opening to the W.S. Press turnings to W.S. on both sides of the opening (*see* Fig. 135).

6. Fit the closed zip into the opening with the zip-tag level with the fitting line. Tack firmly on R.S.

7. Machine all round the opening on the R.S., close to the fold, using a zipper foot (*see* Fig. 136).

THE EDGE-TO-EDGE METHOD

1. Complete the seam up to the base of the opening and press open.

2. Press the turnings to the W.S. on both sides of the opening (*see* Fig. 137).

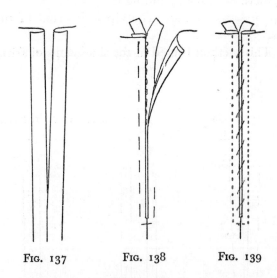

FIG. 137   FIG. 138   FIG. 139

3. Working from the R.S., and with the zip closed and the tag level with the fitting-line, pin one side of the opening to the zip tape so that the fold lies down the centre of the zip teeth. Pin the other side so that the folds meet.

4. Tack firmly down one side and up the other, crossing at the base of the zip teeth (*see* Fig. 138).

5. Catch the folds together with 1 cm tacking-stitches from end to end (*see* Fig. 139).

6. Working on the R.S., machine down one side and up the other, 0·5 cm from the folds, being careful to cross at the bottom just below the end of the zip teeth. Use a zipper foot on the machine (*see* Fig. 139).

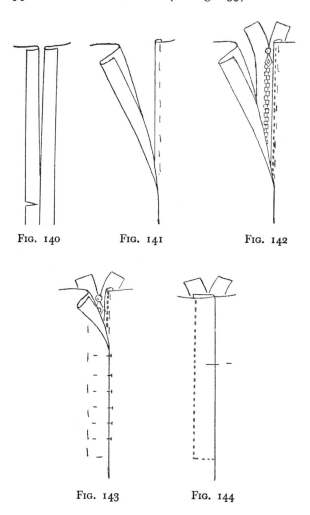

FIG. 140   FIG. 141   FIG. 142

FIG. 143   FIG. 144

The Concealed Method

1. Complete the seam up to the base of the opening and press open.

2. Snip the back turning to the machining, 1 cm below the base of the opening (*see* Fig. 140).

3. Press the front turning to the W.S. on the fitting-line and press the back turning to the W.S., 3 mm outside the fitting-line (*see* Fig. 141).

4. Pin and tack the back turning to the zip tape, with the fold close to but not touching the zip teeth and the tag level with the fitting-line (*see* Fig. 142). Machine close to fold.

5. Bring the front fitting-line over to the back fitting-line and secure with tacking. Tack to tape, 1 cm from the fold (*see* Fig. 143).

6. Machine on the R.S., 1 cm from the fold and cross to the seam at the end of the zip teeth (*see* Fig. 144).

Do not cut the zip tape at either end.

II

Fastenings

THERE are a number of rules that apply to every kind of fastening.

1. With the exception of bound buttonholes and fabric loops, they are all made or applied after the opening has been completed and pressed.

2. They must be suitable for both the type of garment and the material being used.

3. The size of the fastening must be correct for the type of opening and the weight of the material.

4. Fastenings must be sewn on double material.

5. They must be sufficiently close to one another to keep the opening together.

6. They must be opposite to one another so that the opening will lie flat when closed.

Some fastenings, such as hooks and eyes and press-studs, are concealed, but others, such as buttons and buttonholes or buttons and loops, have a decorative value.

BUTTONHOLES

There are three kinds—

1. *Machine-made buttonholes* are strong and quickly made, and are done by using a special attachment on the sewing machine. With a little practice a very presentable buttonhole can be made, and they are particularly suitable for use on overalls and household articles, such as pillowcases. They are made when the garment is otherwise finished.

2. *Hand-worked buttonholes* are used on all but the heaviest materials, but if the material is loosely woven and inclined to fray a backing strip of adhesive interfacing is a great help. The best results are obtained by using mercerized cotton. These buttonholes are worked on the finished garment.

3. *Bound buttonholes* can be done on all except transparent materials, and self or contrasting material can be used for the binding. They are not difficult to do and they wear well. They are always made before the garment is assembled.

All three types can be vertical or horizontal, according to the direction of the strain. On tightly fitting garments and on cuffs the buttonholes must be horizontal, but on loose garments, or where the opening shows a central panel, the buttonholes can be vertical. The latter are always placed on the centre line, and in the case of worked buttonholes both ends are alike.

The size of the buttonhole depends on the size of the button. Measure across the centre of the button and allow 3 mm extra so that the button can slip in and out easily. A very thin button may need less allowance and a thick, elaborate button may need more.

Horizontal buttonholes are marked from the centre line and away from the opening. The distance between the edge of the opening and the buttonhole must be at least half the width of the button, as the edge of the button must not protrude beyond the edge of the opening.

Buttonholes can be evenly spaced or in regular groups.

Worked Buttonholes

1. Mark the length of the buttonholes with two lines of tacking (*see* Fig. 145).

2. Mark each buttonhole along a thread of the material with a fine pencil line (*see* Fig. 145).

3. Work a line of backstitching each side of the mark, 3 mm from the mark (*see* Fig. 146). Do this to every buttonhole before proceeding to the next step. Use the thread you intend to use to work the buttonhole.

4. Cut one buttonhole exactly on the mark, either by using buttonhole scissors or by folding the material and snipping the centre and then cutting to the ends (*see* Fig. 147).

5. Begin working from the end farthest from the opening, working from L. to R. Use the backstitching as a guide for the length of the stitches. Put the needle through the slit and come out just below the backstitching; put the double end of cotton round the point of the needle in the form of a figure eight; pull the needle through and away from you, so that the knot will lie on the raw edge; give an extra little tug so that the knot is quite tight (*see* Figs. 147 and 148). Continue with these stitches, keeping them close together, until you reach the other end.

The round end is worked without twisting the thread round the needle to form knots. Keep the stitches the same length as the buttonhole stitches and

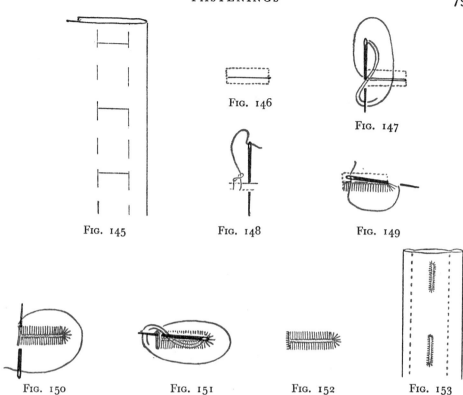

FIG. 146

FIG. 147

FIG. 145

FIG. 148

FIG. 149

FIG. 150

FIG. 151

FIG. 152

FIG. 153

form into a neat half-circle. Work the second side of the buttonhole in the same way as the first (*see* Fig. 149).

The square end is worked by putting your needle through the first knot to draw the buttonhole together; then make three stitches across the width of the buttonhole, and work buttonhole-stitch over these stitches, with the knots towards the slit; fasten off on the W.S. (*see* Figs. 150, 151 and 152).

Vertical buttonholes can be worked with either two round ends or two square ends (*see* Fig. 153).

BOUND BUTTONHOLES

Unlike worked buttonholes, bound buttonholes are made on single material, but a backing strip is helpful and is essential if the material frays badly. There are several methods of making these buttonholes, but the following one is simple and successful.

1. Fix the backing strip to the W.S. of the material, either by means of diagonal tacking or with a hot iron, if the adhesive type is used (*see* Fig. 154).

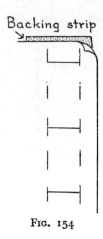

FIG. 154

2. Mark the size of the buttonholes with a double line of tacking and the position of each with a pencil line (*see* Fig. 154).

3. Cut a fabric strip 2·25 cms wide and 2 cms longer than the mark.

4. Fold the strip in half, lengthways, and press; open, and fold and press the edges to meet the central crease (*see* Figs. 155 and 156).

FIG. 155   FIG. 156   FIG. 157

5. Place centre crease of strip over mark, R.S. together, allowing strip to extend 1 cm at each end of mark. Tack firmly (*see* Fig. 157).

6. Machine halfway between fold and centre, each side of the mark, and across the ends (*see* Fig. 158).

7. Cut through centre on the mark, to within 0·5 cm of each end; clip diagonally into the corners (*see* Fig. 159).

8. Turn the strip through to the W.S., letting the folds meet at the centre. (*See* Figs. 160 and 161.)

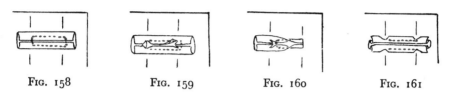

FIG. 158   FIG. 159   FIG. 160   FIG. 161

9. Backstitch the triangle to the strip on the W.S. (*see* Fig. 162).

10. When the facing is in place, cut a slit directly behind the buttonhole, turn under the raw edges and hem to strip (*see* Figs. 163 and 164).

11. For finished buttonhole, see Fig. 165.

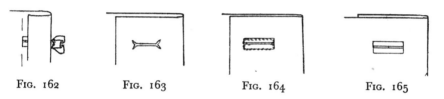

FIG. 162   FIG. 163   FIG. 164   FIG. 165

WORKED LOOPS

This method of fastening is used on faced-slit openings, and is often used on children's clothes. The loops are worked on the right-hand edge of the opening, after it is completed. The size of the loop is gauged by the size of the button; the space across the loop should equal the width of the button.

1. Mark each end of the loop with a pin (*see* Fig. 166).

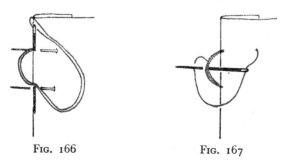

FIG. 166   FIG. 167

2. Using double thread, make a back-stitch into the W.S. of the opening at one pin.

3. Make a tiny stitch in the edge of the opening at the second pin, leaving a loop sufficiently large for the button to pass through. Make a second loop the same size as the first by making a stitch at the first position (*see* Fig. 166).

4. Blanket-stitch the strands together, pushing the stitches tightly against one another (*see* Fig. 167).

FABRIC OR ROULEAU LOOPS

This is a decorative method of fastening and is used on either the C.F. or C.B. of dresses or on fitted, wrist-length sleeves. Small, covered buttons are used with this type of fastening. The loops are made from crossway strips and are called rouleau.

To Make the Rouleau

1. Cut a crossway strip, 2·5 cms wide, and stretch it to its full extent under the iron. This prevents the rouleau from puckering and the machining from breaking.

2. Fold the strip in half lengthways, R.S. inside, and machine 0·25 cm from the fold (*see* Fig. 168).

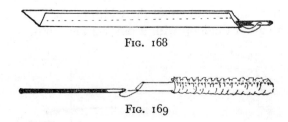

Fig. 168

Fig. 169

3. Trim the turnings to less than the width of the tube.

4. Turn R.S. out, using a bodkin attached with a very short thread to the end of the tube. Press (*see* Fig. 169).

MAKING AND ATTACHING THE LOOPS

Make the loops with the seam on the inner edge. It is optional whether the rouleau is used in one piece or cut into short lengths. The loops should touch one another.

1. Arrange the loops on the R.S. of the fabric, with the distance between the two ends of each loop equalling the width of the button, and the ends of the loops to the edge of the opening. The ends of the loops should overlap slightly (*see* Fig. 170).

2. Pin each loop into position and then tack firmly on the fitting-line.

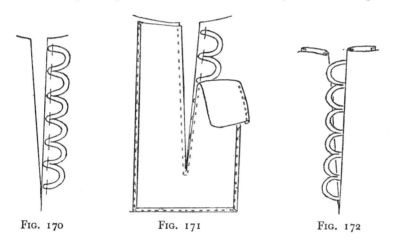

FIG. 170   FIG. 171   FIG. 172

3. Place the R.S. of the facing to the R.S. of the opening, with the loops sandwiched between. Pin and tack on the fitting-line (*see* Fig. 171).

4. Machine on fitting-line; take out all tacking.

5. Turn facing to the W.S. of the opening, tack into position and press (*see* Fig. 172).

BUTTONS

Buttons are sewn on after the buttonholes or loops are completed. They must always be sewn through double material, firmly and strongly. If the button has no shank, one must be made to accommodate the thickness of the buttonhole.

1. Mark the position of the button with crossed pins (*see* Fig. 173).

2. Work by stabbing the needle straight up and down through the holes, leaving the pins in position until you have been through each hole several times.

3. Remove the pins and wind the thread tightly round the strands to form a shank. Fasten off on the W.S. (*see* Fig. 173).

Buttons that have shanks should not be sewn on over pins (*see* Fig. 174).

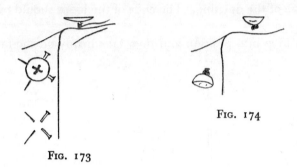

FIG. 174

FIG. 173

HOOKS AND EYES AND HOOKS AND BARS

This is a strong method of fastening and is used in positions where there is some strain, such as skirt waist-bands. Hooks and eyes and bars are available in a number of sizes and in several colours. The hook is sewn to the W.S. of the overlap, so that it is invisible from the R.S., and if there is an underlap a metal or worked bar is sewn on the R.S. of the underlap so that the fitting-lines of the opening lie on top of one another. If the edges of the opening are to meet, then the hook should be sewn 3 mm back from the edge on the W.S. and the eye sewn to the W.S. directly opposite, with the loop of the eye protruding 3 mm beyond the edge.

Locate the position of the hook and hold it in place by working several stitches round the top of the hook and through the material. Bring the thread to the base of the hook and work buttonhole-stitch round both loops (*see* Figs. 175 and 176). The eye or metal bar should also be secured with buttonhole-stitch. Worked bars are made in the same way as worked loops, but are quite flat on the garment (*see* Fig. 167).

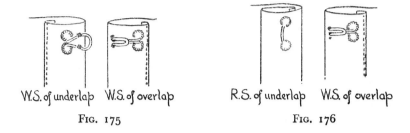

W.S. of underlap W.S. of overlap   R.S. of underlap W.S. of overlap

FIG. 175   FIG. 176

PRESS-STUDS

A popular method of fastening, which is most suitable for use on skirt and dress plackets, where there is very little strain. Secure with buttonhole-stitch, working three stitches in each hole. Sew the knob of the stud to the W.S. of the overlap and the cap directly opposite on the R.S. of the underlap (*see* Fig. 177).

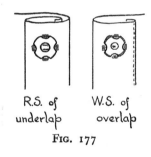

R.S. of   W.S. of
underlap overlap

FIG. 177

12
Hems

A HEM is a method of neatening a raw edge. Unless it is secured with a decorative stitch, it should be invisible on the R.S. and neat and perfectly even on the W.S.

The width of the hem varies according to its position, the shape of the edge, and the material used. The average width of a hem on a skirt or dress that is straight or gathered is 8 cms, but if the skirt is shaped or flared the hem must be narrower. On a fully circular skirt the hem should not be more than 1 cm wide.

THE HEM ON THE LOWER EDGE OF A GARMENT

The garment must be otherwise completed, including fastenings and belt, before the hem is attempted. If the garment has a shaped skirt it should be hung for 48 hours before the hem is made.

LEVELLING

1. Put the garment on, wearing the correct undergarments and shoes.
2. Stand on a table so that the fitter can both see and work more easily. Stand upright but not stiffly and let the fitter move round you.
3. Using either a T-square or a "Pin-it" hem leveller, measure from the table to the required level. Pins are more accurate than chalk (*see* Fig. 178).
4. Mark on all the seams and every seven centimetres between.

TURNING UP

1. Lay the garment on the table, W.S. uppermost, and the hem towards you.
2. Fold the hem to the W.S. on the marked line, keeping the seam straight; pin as you go.
3. Tack 2 cms from the fold and press.

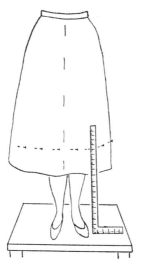

FIG. 178

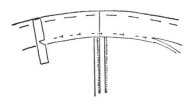

FIG. 179

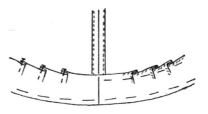

FIG. 180

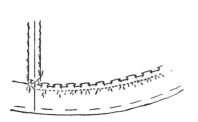

FIG. 181

FIG. 182

4. Using a gauge, a ruler, or a tape with a stiff end, measure from the fold the required width of the hem. Mark with chalk and cut away the surplus (*see* Fig. 179).

5. If the hem lies quite flat, turn the raw edge under 0·5 cm, tack and press.

6. Slip-hem to secure.

If the skirt is shaped, there will be a certain amount of fullness to be dealt with. When using cotton or any other thin, non-shrinking material, the surplus fullness must be formed into tiny pleats, which are held in place with the hemming (*see* Fig. 180). If the material is wool, the fullness can be gathered and shrunk away before the edge is finished (*see* Figs. 181 and 182).

The Pleated Hem that Includes a Seam

1. Snip the seam turning at the depth of the hem and press open below snip.
2. Turn hem up in the usual way and re-press the pleat (*see* Fig. 183).

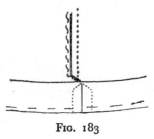

Fig. 183

HEM FINISHES

The Edge Turned Under and Slip-hemmed

This is the most usual method and is suitable on all thin materials.

1. When the hem has been trimmed to an even depth, turn the raw edge under 0·5 cm. Pin and tack to the garment.

2. Press well. The hem should not be pressed after the hemming is done.

3. Slip-hem. Begin in the fold of the hem, then pick up one thread of the single material immediately underneath and close to the fold. Put the needle back into the fold, close to where the thread came out and slip it along inside the fold. Do not pull the stitches tightly (*see* Fig. 184 *a* and *b*).

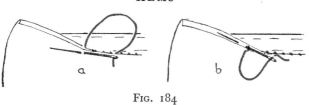

Fig. 184

A Hem Finished with Paris Binding

This method is used on heavy woollens, such as tweeds.

1. The hem should be trimmed to an even depth and pressed well.
2. Pin and tack a piece of Paris binding to the R.S. of the material, with one edge of the binding extending just beyond the edge of the material.

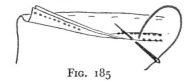

Fig. 185

3. Machine close to the lower edge of the binding.
4. Tack to the garment and hem invisibly (*see* Fig. 185).

A Hem Finished with Bias Binding

This is a very neat finish and is used on fine and medium-weight woollens.

1. The hem should be trimmed, and also gathered and shrunk if necessary.
2. Place the R.S. of the bias strip to the R.S. of the edge of the hem. Pin, tack and machine, 0·5 cm from the edge.

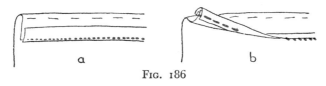

Fig. 186

3. Press the binding up and over the raw edge. Hold in position by stab-stitching along the seam. The stitches should not show on the R.S. but can be 0·5 cm long on the W.S.

4. Press the binding, pin, tack, and slip-hem to the garment (*see* Fig. 186 *a* and *b*).

A Hem Finished with Herringbone Stitch

This method of finishing is most suitable on jersey cloths, because they do not fray but they do stretch across the width, and herringbone is an elastic stitch.

    1. Turn the hem up in the usual way, tack and press flat.

    2. Secure with fine herringbone stitches, making sure that the stitches on the single material do not show through to the R.S. (*see* Fig. 187).

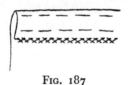

Fig. 187

A Hem Finished with Edge-stitching

This finish is suitable for heavy silks and materials with a vertical rib.

    1. Prepare the hem in the usual way but instead of turning the raw edge under, machine close to the edge, and press.

    2. Catch the edge very lightly to the garment.

THE FALSE HEM

A garment can be lengthened by a false hem.

    1. Unpick the existing hem and press flat. If the garment has to be washed, it is a good idea to unpick before washing so that special attention can be given to the fold mark. If the skirt is a shaped one, it may be necessary to straighten it (follow the instructions for levelling given on page 86).

    2. Cut a strip of the same material, or one of similar weight and colour, long enough to fit round the edge of the garment, plus turnings, and four inches wide. Join it into a circle and press the seam open.

    3. Place the R.S. of the strip to the R.S. of the garment with the edges together. Pin, tack and machine 1 cm from the edge. Press the seam open.

4. Fold the hem to the W.S., with the seam 1 cm above the fold on the W.S. of the garment. Press and finish as for ordinary hem (*see* Fig. 188). Cut the strip narrower and on the cross if the skirt is shaped.

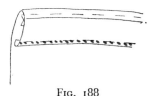

FIG. 188

THE NARROW HEM

Narrow hems are often used on underwear and nightwear and can be secured by means of machining or hand-stitching. The hand finish can be slip-hemming, shell hemming, rolling and whipping, pin-stitching and hemstitching. Where narrow hems are needed when attaching lace (*see* page 136) pin-stitching or hemstitching may be used instead of slip-hemming.

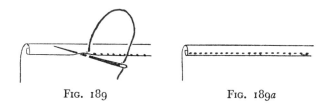

FIG. 189   FIG. 189*a*

1. Turn the whole hem allowance to the W.S. and press.
2. Turn raw edge under and tack and press.
3. Machine close to inner fold or slip-hem (*see* Figs. 189 and 189*a*).

SHELL HEMMING

1. Work two slip-hemming stitches, then take the thread over the hem twice, pulling these two stitches firmly.
2. Continue in this way, forming a scalloped edge (*see* Fig. 190).

ROLLING AND WHIPPING

This finish can be used only on very fine, soft materials and sheers.

1. Using the forefinger and thumb, roll the raw edge towards you.

2. Hold the roll in place with fine whipping stitches as you go (*see* Fig. 191).

FIG. 190   FIG. 191

PIN-STITCHING

Turn the hem to the R.S.

Use mercerized sewing cotton and a size 2 needle. The thick needle is essential for punching holes in the material.

1. Make a back-stitch in the single material, immediately below the hem.

2. Put the needle through the first hole and bring it out in the hem over the second hole.

3. Return the needle to the second hole and make a running stitch in the single material.

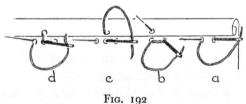

d   c   b   a

FIG. 192

4. Repeat from 1., making sure that the needle enters the previous hole each time and that the thread is drawn tightly, so that a row of holes is obtained close to the hem (*see* Fig. 192).

Pin-stitching can be used to attach lace to an edge, and as a decorative method of working a seam.

HEMSTITCHING

This is a decorative method of securing a hem. It is necessary that the material should be evenly woven, linens give the best results. The thread used should be of similar thickness to the threads of the material.

1. Draw the required number of threads and turn up the hem so that it is level with the drawn threads (*see* Fig. 193*a*).

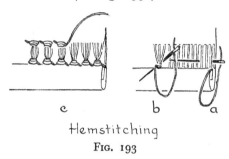

Hemstitching

FIG. 193

2. Working from the W.S. secure the thread in the hem. Pick up three threads (*see* Fig. 193*a*) then pass the needle behind the same threads a second time and into the hem (*see* Fig. 193*b*).

3. Work along the hem grouping the threads into even bundles.

4. Turn the work upside down and work back along the other edge of the drawn threads (*see* Fig. 193*c*).

THE MITRED CORNER

It is sometimes necessary to turn a corner when neatening an edge with a hem and the neatest way of doing this is to mitre it.

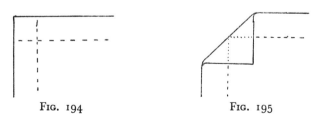

FIG. 194   FIG. 195

1. Press the hem allowance on both edges to the W.S. Open out (*see* Fig. 194).

2. Fold the corner over diagonally where the creases cross (*see* Fig. 195).

3. Trim off corner to 3 mm from the fold (*see* Fig. 196).

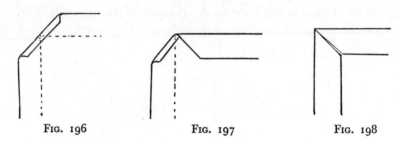

FIG. 196   FIG. 197   FIG. 198

4. Re-fold hems on the original creases (*see* Figs. 197 and 198).

5. Turn under the raw edges to neaten and slip-stitch the diagonal folds together. Finish by hemming or machining.

13
Collars

COLLARS are always fashionable, and can vary in size and shape tremendously, but the method of making them is always very similar. They are usually made from double material and are often interfaced to give them a smooth and crisp appearance.

BASIC STYLES

The Peter Pan Collar lies quite flat on the garment, which is fastened up to the neck; it is popular on children's garments (*see* Fig. 199). *The Rever Collar* is straighter and stands up at the back. It can be worn open, or fastened up to the

FIG. 199   FIG. 200

neck (*see* Fig. 200). These two collars are the basic shapes from which most of the variations stem.

There is a third type, called the *Roll* or *Extended front* collar, where the collar is cut in one with the facings and the collar facing is cut in one with the bodice front.

MAKING A COLLAR

1. Stick or tack the interfacing to the W.S. of the undercollar.
2. Place the two collar pieces, R.S. together, with C.B. matching and the notches on the neck edge matching.
3. Pin, tack and machine all round the outside edge on the fitting-line, leaving the neck edge free.
4. Trim the turnings to 0·5 cm, snip off corners and notch the curves (*see* Figs. 201*a* and 202*a*).

5. Turn collar R.S. out and pull corners out with a pin. Tack close to the seam, rolling it between the finger and thumb to prevent a groove forming (*see* Figs. 199 and 200).

6. Press well.

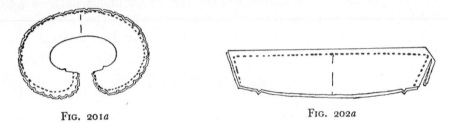

FIG. 201*a*   FIG. 202*a*

To Attach a Collar: Method I

1. The shoulder seams of the bodice must be completed, neatened, and pressed and the free edge of the facings neatened.

2. Place the underside of the collar to the R.S. of the garment, with C.B. and notches matching. The front edge of the collar should come to the C.F. of the garment (*see* Fig. 201*b*).

FIG. 201*b*   FIG. 202*b*

3. Tack firmly, using small stitches.

4. Fold the front facings back on top of the collar, matching the notches. Tack firmly (*see* Fig. 202*b*).

5. Cut a crossway strip, 2·5 cms wide and about 17·5 cms long.

6. Place the crossway strip over the collar and overlapping the facings about 2 cms. Tack firmly on the fitting-line.

7. Machine on the fitting-line from one front fold to the other (*see* Fig. 203).

8. Trim the turnings to 0·5 cm, snip curve and cut off corners.

9. Turn the facings back to the W.S. of the garment and pull the collar out until the seam is flat on both sides. Tack and press.

10. Turn under the free edge of the crossway strip and pin and hem to the garment. Catch the edge of the facing to the crossway strip (*see* Fig. 204).

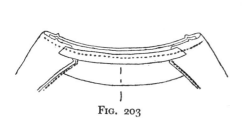

FIG. 203

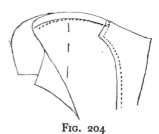

FIG. 204

TO ATTACH A COLLAR: METHOD 2

1. Turn the facings to the R.S. on the fold-line. Pin, tack and machine from the fold to the C.F. (*see* Fig. 205).

2. Snip the turning at the C.F. to the end of the machining. Trim the turnings and snip off the corners (*see* Fig. 205).

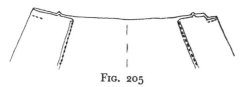

FIG. 205

3. Turn the facing to the W.S. of the garment and press.

4. Pin the top side of the collar to the W.S. of the garment, matching C.B. and notches. Front edges of collar should come to C.F. of garment.

5. Tack and machine the single thickness of collar to the neckline of the garment on the fitting-line (*see* Fig. 206).

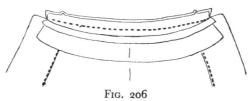

FIG. 206

6. Remove tacking, trim turnings to 0·5 cm and snip curves.

7. Fold under the raw edge of the under-collar, pin to stitch-line and hem (*see* Fig. 207).

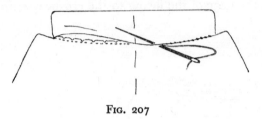

FIG. 207

ROLL COLLARS

1. Pin, tack and machine the seam at the C.B. of the collar on the fitting-line. Press open (*see* Fig. 208).

2. Work the seam at the C.B. of the facing in the same way (*see* Fig. 209).

3. Strengthen the corner at the neck edge of the shoulder by machining on the fitting-line (*see* Fig. 208). Snip corners (*see* Fig. 210*a* and *b*).

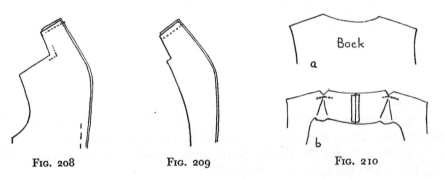

FIG. 208   FIG. 209   FIG. 210

4. Pin B. and F. shoulders, R.S. together, on the fitting-line. Match C.B. of collar to C.B. of garment and pin across neck edge on the fitting-line. Tack firmly.

5. Machine on the fitting-line, beginning at one shoulder edge and finishing at the other. Work from collar side (*see* Fig. 211).

6. Press shoulder seams open. Snip and press neck seam towards collar (*see* Fig. 212).

7. Place R.S. of collar to R.S. of facing. Pin, tack and machine round outer edge (*see* Fig. 213).

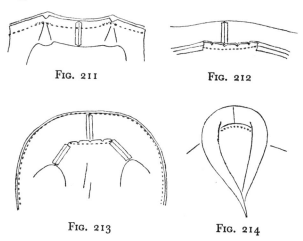

FIG. 211

FIG. 212

FIG. 213

FIG. 214

8. Trim turnings and snip curves. Turn the facing to the W.S. of the garment, tack close to the seam and press.

9. Turn under the neck edge of the facing and pin and hem to the back neck seam (*see* Fig. 214).

14
Cuffs

Cuffs are usually designed so that they are the same shape as the collar on the free or outside edge.

The cuff should be made and attached to the sleeve-end before the sleeve is set into the garment. It can be either a simple, circular band or a shaped cuff that turns back over the sleeve. If the sleeve is wrist-length, then an opening and fastenings are needed, but these are sometimes dispensed with on three-quarter-length sleeves.

PREPARATION OF SLEEVE

The opening should be completed and the seam machined, neatened and pressed. If it is a gathered sleeve then two rows of fine gathering must be worked round the sleeve-end, one on the fitting-line and the second 0·5 cm outside.

METHOD OF MAKING THE CIRCULAR BAND (no sleeve opening)

1. Join the two short sides of the cuff piece to form a circle, and press the seam open (*see* Figs. 215, 216, 217).

2. Press the cuff in half with the R.S. outside (*see* Fig. 218).

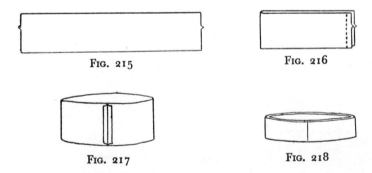

FIG. 215

FIG. 216

FIG. 217

FIG. 218

3. Pull up the gathers on the sleeve-end until it fits the cuff; wind the threads round a pin, and distribute the gathers evenly (*see* Fig. 219).

4. Place the R.S. of the cuff (single material) to the R.S. of the sleeve-end, with the seams matching. Pin, tack, and machine on the fitting-line, working from the gathered side (*see* Fig. 220).

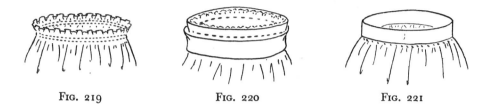

FIG. 219   FIG. 220   FIG. 221

5. Remove tacking and trim the turnings to 0·5 cm.

6. Turn under the free edge of the cuff and pin to the stitch-line. Hem to machine stitches and press (*see* Fig. 221).

METHOD OF MAKING THE TURNED-BACK CUFF (no opening and sleeve ungathered)

1. Place the two cuff pieces, R.S. together; pin, tack and machine round the outer edge on the fitting-line (*see* Fig. 222).

2. Trim the turnings, snip the corners, or notch the curves; turn R.S. out and press.

3. Pin and tack both layers of the cuff to the sleeve-end, with the underside of the cuff to the R.S. of the sleeve and the notches matching.

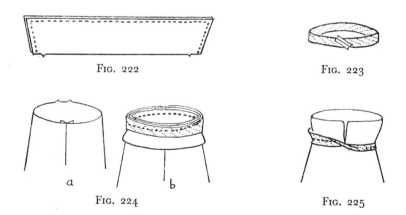

FIG. 222   FIG. 223

FIG. 224   FIG. 225

4. Cut a crossway strip, 2·5 cms wide and long enough to encircle the sleeve end. Join into a circle (*see* Fig. 223).

5. Place R.S. of strip on top of the cuff and pin, tack and machine all layers together on the fitting-line (*see* Fig. 224).

6. Trim turnings to 0·5 cm and pull the cuff up from the sleeve; turn the strip to the W.S. of the sleeve. Tack and press.

7. Turn under the free edge of the strip and hem to sleeve (*see* Fig. 225).

METHOD OF MAKING THE CUFF FOR A SLEEVE WITH AN OPENING

1. Fold the cuff piece in half lengthways, R.S. inside, and machine across the ends on the fitting-lines. Stop machining as indicated in the diagram (*see* Fig. 226*a*).

2. Trim the turnings and turn cuff R.S. out and press (*see* Fig. 226*b*).

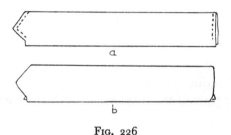

FIG. 226

3. Place the R.S. of the cuff (single material) to the R.S. of the sleeve, with the ends of the cuff in line with the edges of the opening. The pointed end of the cuff should match with the overlap edge of the opening.

4. Pin, tack and machine on the fitting-line, working from the gathered side (*see* Fig. 227*a* and *b*).

5. Take out tacking and trim the turnings to 0·5 cm.

6. Fold under the free edge of the cuff, pin and hem to stitch-line. Press (*see* Fig. 228).

7. Work a buttonhole on the pointed end of the cuff and sew a button on the other end (*see* Fig. 228).

If the cuff is to be fastened with links, the sleeve opening should be a faced slit and both ends of the cuff alike. Work a buttonhole on both ends (*see* Fig. 229).

FIG. 227

FIG. 228

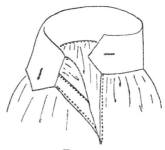

FIG. 229

LINKED BUTTONS

Using double thread and holding the two buttons about 1 cm apart, join them with several strands. Blanket-stitch over the strands, pushing the stitches close together (*see* Fig. 230).

FIG. 230

15
Sleeves

SET-IN sleeves are never out of fashion, and therefore it is important to know how to fit them into the armhole really well. It is necessary to be very accurate when working the shoulder seam, the underarm seam, and the sleeve seam. If care is not taken over these seams the sleeve-head will not be the correct size for the armhole. The sleeves are usually set into the garment after the neck has been completed and before the bodice and skirt are joined together. Complete the lower edge of the sleeve before setting it into the armhole. There is a little more shaping on the back of the sleeve-head than on the front, to allow for arm movement; therefore it is important that the sleeves should be made up as a pair. The notches should help you to check this.

The sleeve-head is about 2 cms–3 cms larger than the armhole, to allow for the curve and movement of the shoulder.

METHOD OF SETTING IN SLEEVES

1. Run a gathering thread round the head of the sleeve on the fitting-line, beginning at the back notches and finishing at the front notches; leave the end hanging. Work a second row, 0·5 cm outside (*see* Fig. 231).

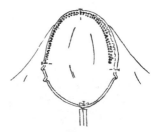

FIG. 231   FIG. 232

2. Place the L. sleeve to the L. armhole, R.S. together, with underarm seams and notches matching. Pin on the fitting-line, working from the sleeve side (*see* Fig. 232).

3. Pull up the gathering threads until the sleeve-head fits the armhole; wind the threads round a pin and distribute the gathers evenly.

4. Still working from the sleeve side, pin the rest of the sleeve to the armhole, on the fitting-line.

5. Test the hang of the sleeve by holding the shoulder over your hand; it should hang down straight or a little forward (*see* Fig. 233).

6. Tack round the armhole, from the sleeve side, on the fitting-line, using small stitches (*see* Fig. 234).

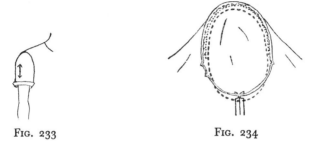

FIG. 233   FIG. 234

7. Try the garment on at this stage to see whether the shoulder is the right length and the armhole seam a smooth curve.

8. Machine on fitting-line from sleeve side.

9. Remove tacking and trim the turnings to *not* less than 1 cm.

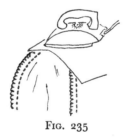

FIG. 235

10. Neaten by blanket-stitching both turnings together. Press towards sleeve (*see* Fig. 235).

The turnings may be neatened by binding if the material frays badly; this method is also used on housecoats and unlined jackets. Another method of neatening, used on nightwear, is to trim the sleeve-turning to half, then roll the armhole-turning over it and hem it to the stitch-line. This method stands up well to frequent laundering.

THE RAGLAN SLEEVE

A garment with a raglan sleeve fits more loosely than one with a set-in sleeve, and is therefore particularly suitable for raincoats and top-coats that are worn over suits. The diagonal line from the underarm to the neck does not suit every type of figure, particularly people with very sloping shoulders (*see* Fig. 236).

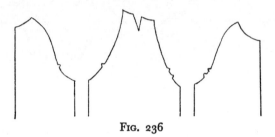

FIG. 236

The shoulder seam is replaced by a dart and the diagonal seams are often accentuated by the use of a decorative seam, such as the lapped seam or the double-stitched seam.

METHOD OF MAKING THE RAGLAN SLEEVE

1. Work the dart at the head of the sleeve and press open or to the back (*see* Fig. 237).

2. Join the front edge of the sleeve to the front of the bodice, matching notches. Both these edges are bias-cut, so care must be taken not to stretch them. Snip the seam turnings where they curve, and press (*see* Fig. 238).

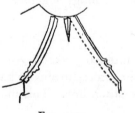

FIG. 237   FIG. 238

3. Join the back edge of the sleeve to the back of the bodice in the same way (*see* Fig. 237).

4. Pin back and front side seams together and continue pinning along the sleeve seam.

5. Machine on the fitting-line, snip on curve, neaten and press (*see* Fig. 238).

THE DOLMAN OR KIMONO SLEEVE

This sleeve is cut in one with the B. and F. of the bodice, and the shoulder seam extends down the whole length of the sleeve. It is loose fitting and comfortable to wear, but as there is some strain on the underarm seam, jersey materials, which are elastic, are the most suitable to use.

The underarm seam is either curved or angled, or a gusset is used. The latter is the most satisfactory, as particular care must be taken to strengthen the curve or angle to prevent the garment splitting across.

THE CURVED UNDERARM SEAM (PLAIN SEAM)

1. Cut 4 crossway strips, 3 cms wide and 10 cms long.

2. Turn 0·5 cm turnings to the W.S. on one edge of each strip and tack into position on each of the 4 bodice pieces, as shown in Fig. 239.

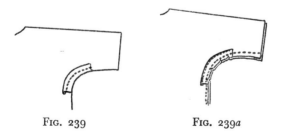

FIG. 239   FIG. 239a

3. Machine close to the fold.

4. Place the R.S. of the back and front sections together, pin, tack and machine on the fitting-line. Snip curve, neaten and press (*see* Fig. 239a).

The Curved Underarm Seam (French Seam)

1. Prepare crossway strips as above, but turn under both edges.
2. With W.S. of B. and F. sections together, work the first row of machining, trim turnings and snip curve (*see* Fig. 240).
3. Prepare seam for second row of machining and tack the strip into position, with one fold on the fitting-line, and the other fold tacked to single material.
4. Machine seam and inner fold of strip (*see* Fig. 240*a*).

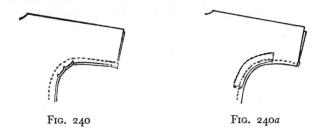

FIG. 240   FIG. 240*a*

For "Angled Underarm Seam" *see* Figs. 86, 87 and 88, page 60.

THE GUSSET IN AN UNDERARM SEAM

A gusset is usually square or diamond-shaped, with the direct cross of the material running from corner to corner across the centre of the gusset. That is the reason why it takes the strain so well (*see* Fig. 241).

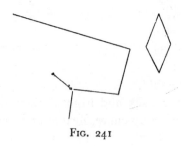

FIG. 241

METHOD OF INSERTING THE GUSSET

1. Transfer the slash marks to the material and machine round the mark, 3 mm away (*see* Fig. 242).

2. Cut between the stitching, almost to the point (*see* Fig. 243).

3. Pin, tack and machine the sleeve and underarm seams. Press open and neaten (*see* Fig. 244).

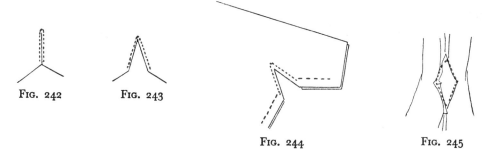

FIG. 242   FIG. 243   FIG. 244   FIG. 245

4. Pin and tack the gusset to the slashed edges, R.S. together.

5. Machine from sleeve seam to underarm seam along both sides of the gusset (*see* Fig. 245).

6. Press the seam away from the gusset and edge-stitch on the R.S.

16

Facings

A FACING is a method of neatening an edge that shows on one side only (*see* Fig. 242). Facings turned to the R.S. are decorative and can be finished with one or more rows of machining or with an embroidery stitch. A crossway strip can be used as a facing, but should not be more than 2 cms wide when finished (*see* Fig. 246c). Facings other than crossway facings must be cut the same shape,

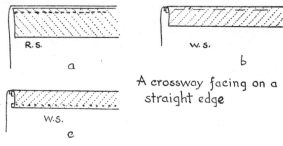

A crossway facing on a
straight edge

FIG. 246

size and grain as the edge to be faced. Neck and armhole facings have seams corresponding to those on the garment.

METHOD OF MAKING THE NECK FACING ON THE W.S. OF THE GARMENT

1. Work the shoulder seams of the garment, neaten and press.
2. Pin, tack and machine the shoulder seams of the facing on the fitting-line. Press open.
3. Neaten the outer edge of the facing by turning 0·5 cm to the W.S. and machining close to the fold. Press.
4. Place the R.S. of the facing to the R.S. of the garment, matching the shoulder seams and notches. Pin, tack and machine on the fitting-line (*see* Fig. 247).
5. Remove the tacking, trim the turnings to 0·5 cm, snip the curves. If the neck is square, snip into the corners, and if it is a vee neck, snip into the vee (*see* Figs. 248 and 249).

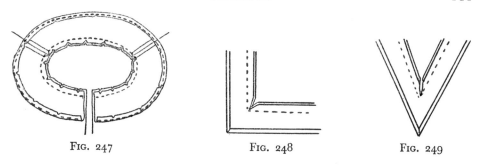

FIG. 247   FIG. 248   FIG. 249

6. Turn the facing to the W.S. of the garment and tack close to the seam, making sure that the facing does not show on the R.S. (*see* Fig. 250).

7. Press well and catch the facing to the shoulder seams.

Armhole facings are worked in the same way (*see* Fig. 251).

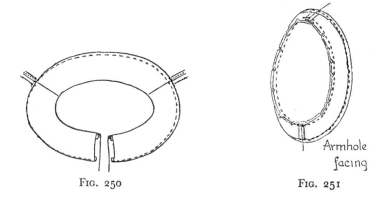

FIG. 250   FIG. 251

METHOD OF MAKING NECK FACING ON THE R.S. OF THE GARMENT

The shoulder seams of the garment must be reversed at the finished width of the facing from the neck. This is done to prevent the shoulder turnings from showing at the neck edge.

TO REVERSE THE SHOULDER SEAMS

1. Place B. and F. shoulders, R.S. together, and pin on the fitting-line. Measure from neck edge the finished width of the facing and mark.

2. Tack and machine from the mark to the shoulder edge. Tie off ends.

3. Snip turnings at mark to end of machining (*see* Fig. 252).

4. Reverse the seam and machine to neck edge on the fitting-line (*see* Fig. 253).

5. Press the seam flat on both sides and trim off the corners on the R.S. (*see* Fig. 254).

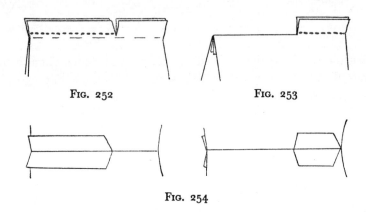

FIG. 252　　　　　　　　　　　FIG. 253

FIG. 254

The neck edge of the decorative facing must be the same size and shape as the neck edge of the garment, but the outer edge can be cut to any desired shape, e.g. scalloped.

MAKING AND APPLYING THE FACING

1. Pin, tack and machine the shoulder seams of the facing on the fitting-line. Press open.

2. Turn the outer edge of the facing to the W.S. on the fitting-line; tack and press. If the edge is scalloped, snip into the corner of each scallop and tack with small stitches so that a smooth line is retained (*see* Fig. 255).

3. Place the R.S. of the facing to the W.S. of the garment, matching the seams and notches. Pin, tack and machine on the fitting-line.

4. Trim the turnings to 0·5 cm and snip the curves (*see* Fig. 255).

5. Turn the facing to the R.S. of the garment and tack the neckline so that the seam is just a thread to the W.S. Press.

6. Pin and tack the facing into position on the garment, still keeping the seams in line (*see* Fig. 256).

7. Secure with machining or an embroidery stitch.

The facings on short and three-quarter sleeves are done in the same way.

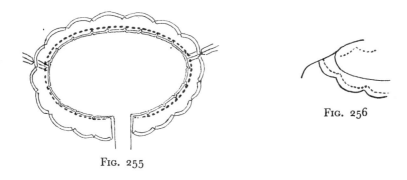

FIG. 256

FIG. 255

FACING WITH A CROSSWAY STRIP

This is often used with very pleasing effect on checked material. For a square neck, cut four strips of crossway material (the width will depend on the size of the checks) and allow 0·5 cm turnings on both edges. Cut each strip long enough to fit one edge of the neckline, plus turnings. Each end of the strips must be cut along a thread, so that the facing will form a square when the corners are joined (*see* Figs. 257 and 258). Apply the facing in the same way as the previous one.

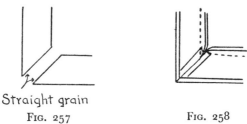

Straight grain

FIG. 257   FIG. 258

17
Waistbands and Belts

THE seams of the skirt must be finished, neatened and pressed, and the opening completed, before the waistband is put on. The waistband will look better and feel more comfortable if a fairly stiff interlining is used. Petersham is often used for this purpose but a strip of canvas or one of the bonded interfacings will do quite well. The strip of material for the waistband must be cut on the straight grain. The interfacing should be the same length as the waistband and the exact finished width of the band.

TO MAKE THE WAISTBAND

1. Fold the strip of material in half lengthways, with W.S. inside (*see* Fig. 259). Press.

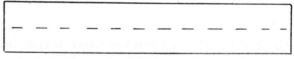

FIG. 259

2. Open the strip out and pin the interfacing to the W.S. with one edge along the crease. Secure with diagonal tacking (*see* Fig. 260).

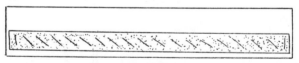

FIG. 260

3. Fold the turning over the edge of the interfacing, tack and press.
4. Fold band lengthways, with R.S. inside, and machine across the ends on the fitting-lines (*see* Fig. 261).

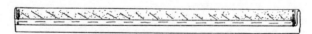

FIG. 261

5. Trim the turnings and turn band R.S. out. Press well (*see* Fig. 262).

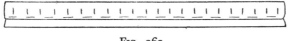

FIG. 262

TO APPLY THE BAND TO THE SKIRT WAIST

1. Place the R.S. of the band to the R.S. of the skirt, using the unstiffened side of the band. One end of the band should be in line with the front edge of the opening and the other end in line with the edge of the underlap.

2. Pin, tack and machine on the fitting-line (*see* Fig. 263).

3. Remove tacks, tie off ends and trim turnings slightly.

4. Fold the finished edge of the band over to the W.S. of the skirt; pin the fold to the stitch line and hem (*see* Fig. 264).

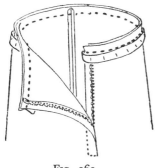

FIG. 263

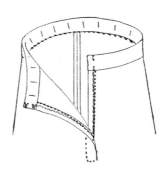

FIG. 264

THE STIFFENED BELT

Cut a strip of material, on the straight grain, twice the finished width of the belt, plus turnings, and fifteen centimetres longer than the waist measurement. Cut a strip of interfacing the exact finished width of the belt and the same length.

METHOD OF MAKING THE STIFFENED BELT

1. Fold the strip of material in half lengthways, R.S. out, and press.

2. Open it out and pin the interfacing to the W.S., with the edge to the crease. Secure with diagonal tacks (*see* Fig. 265).

3. Fold the turnings to the W.S. all round. Mitre the turnings at the pointed end. Press well (*see* Fig. 266).

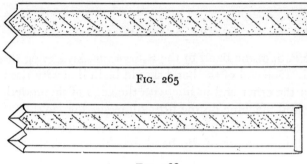

Fig. 265

Fig. 266

4. Fold the belt in half, R.S. out, and tack the edges together.

5. Machine close to the edge all round the belt. Press (*see* Fig. 267).

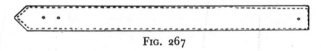

Fig. 267

6. Make an eyelet hole 3 cms from the straight end, to take the prong of the buckle, and eyelets at the other end, to give the correct waist size. It is possible to buy outfits for fixing metal eyelets; these are easy to use and very satisfactory.

To Work Eyelet Holes

1. Mark the position of the hole.

2. Work a circle of tiny running-stitches round the mark. If the belt is thick, stab-stitching is easier than running-stitch (*see* Fig. 269).

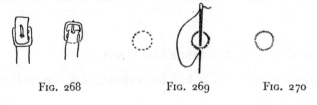

Fig. 268   Fig. 269   Fig. 270

3. Pierce a hole in the centre of the circle with a stiletto or a knitting needle.

4. Work round the hole with small, tight oversewing stitches (*see* Figs. 269 and 270).

To Make the Tie Belt

1. Cut a strip of material, twice the finished width of the belt, plus turnings, by the required length.

2. Fold in half lengthways, R.S. inside. Pin and tack.

3. Machine the edges together, including both ends, but leave about 7 cms in the centre unstitched (*see* Fig. 271).

4. Trim the turnings, snip off the corners and turn the belt R.S. out.

5. Press and slip-stitch the folds together in the centre (*see* Fig. 272).

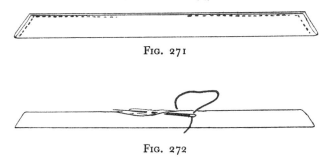

FIG. 271

FIG. 272

To Work the Belt Carriers

The belt carriers should be worked one on each side seam, and should be big enough just to take the belt comfortably. With matching thread, work four strands on the R.S. of the garment so that the belt will be held in position on the waist-line (*see* Figs. 273*a*, *b*, *c*). Blanket-stitch the strands together very closely.

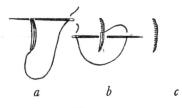

a   *b*   *c*

FIG. 273

18
Pockets

THE PATCH POCKETS

1. The fold lines are shown in Fig. 274.

2. Fold a 0·5 cm turning to the W.S. on the top edge of the pocket and machine (*see* Fig. 275).

3. Fold the complete hem allowance at the top of the pocket to the R.S. and machine on the fitting-line each side to the depth of the hem (*see* Fig. 276).

4. Snip off the corners and turn the hem to the W.S. Press.

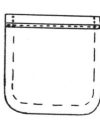

Fig. 274   Fig. 275   Fig. 276

5. Press the turnings on the remaining edges to the W.S. If the bottom corners are square they must be mitred. If they are rounded the turnings must be notched (*see* Fig. 277).

Fig. 277   Fig. 278

6. Pin and tack the pocket into position on the garment and machine close to the edge, strengthening the top corners with a triangle or a square of machine stitching (*see* Fig. 278).

PATCH POCKETS WITH TURNED-DOWN CUFFS

1. Allow twice the required depth of the cuff, extra to the top hem allowance.

2. Follow the instructions above for making up the pocket.

3. When the pocket is tacked into position, start and finish machining at the required depth of the cuff.

4. Press the cuff down over the pocket.

POCKETS IN SEAMS

1. Matching the notches on the pocket pieces with those on the side seams, place one pocket piece R.S. together with the skirt front and the other R.S. together with the back skirt (*see* Fig. 279).

2. Machine on the fitting-line, leaving the seam allowance at the top and bottom of the pocket pieces unstitched (*see* Fig. 279).

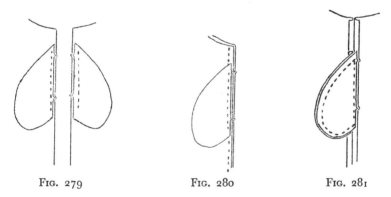

FIG. 279   FIG. 280   FIG. 281

3. Complete the skirt seams above and below the pocket. Press. (*See* Fig. 280).

4. Machine the free edges of the pocket pieces together and press towards the front of the skirt (*see* Fig. 281).

19
Embroidery

MOST people, at some time or another, have been sufficiently attracted by the beauty created by the skilled combination of fabric, thread and stitch, which is embroidery, to attempt the craft themselves. The gifted ones go on and produce articles that are admired by everyone who sees them, but others, because they have not grasped the basic principles, are discouraged and feel that this delightful accomplishment is not for them.

As with all crafts, it is necessary to have the right tools, and fortunately these are simple and can be easily obtained.

EQUIPMENT

Crewel needles—an assortment of sizes; it is important to use the right size, as too large a needle makes holes in the material.

Tapestry needles—blunt-tipped needles for canvas work.

Cottons, silks, and wools.

Sharp-pointed embroidery scissors.

Pencil and ruler.

Carbon and tracing-paper.

The next thing is to know what threads are available, what their individual characteristics are, and how and where they can be used and combined to the best effect. There are no absolute rules about the choice of thread and material; most threads can be used on most materials, though it is usual to use silk on silk. Silk thread can also be used on linen and synthetic fabrics, and the lustre of silk thread combined with the dull surface of wool gives a very pleasing effect. The one thing to be careful about is that the weight or thickness of the thread and the material balance. Do not attempt to pull a thick thread through fine material; if a thick thread is needed for the design it must be couched.

THREADS

Coton-à-broder   Medium fine, easy to use, suitable for medium-weight fabrics; often used for drawn-thread work.

Stranded cotton Can be divided to suit different weights of material; excellent for satin stitch and long and short, because it gives a smooth effect.

Soft embroidery Thick cotton thread; it can be couched on almost any fabric but can be taken through only loosely woven materials such as canvas, hessian and java cloth.

Filoselle Stranded silk, used on silks and synthetics, and sometimes combined with dull, surfaced threads for effect.

Crewel wool Fine and adaptable; used on medium-weight linen, cotton, and woollen materials. Excellent for Jacobean work.

Tapestry wool A thicker wool, suitable for canvas work.

There is a large range of suitable materials from which to choose; the following lists mention a few.

MATERIALS

Linen This is the most popular embroidery fabric. It can be obtained in a number of different weights, from handkerchief linen to suiting linen. It varies, too, in weave, from the smooth, tightly woven table-linen to the more loosely woven canvas and crash. Linen is not cheap, but it is hard wearing and is obtainable in many widths, from 45 cms to 180 cms, which makes it economical to use.

It is suitable for making table- and tray-cloths, runners, chair-backs and cushion-covers, among other things. Almost any thread can be used on linen.

Linen is available in white, natural and a variety of colours.

Cotton There are many cotton materials suitable for embroidery, some of which look very like linen. Imitation linen is less expensive than linen.

Java and Sumatra canvas, denim, casement, sailcloth, gingham, cambric are all fabrics suitable for making beach-bags, aprons, place-mats, cushion-covers, etc. Single- and double-thread canvas are both suitable for chair-seats and fire-screens. Wool or soft embroidery thread is used on them. Crash, made from a mixture of cotton and jute, is used for cushion-covers and runners. Cotton threads are most suitable.

Wool   Flannel, light-weight dress fabric, felt and tweed are all woollens. Flannel makes a cot or pram cover. Dress fabric makes stoles, scarves and cushion-covers. Felt and tweed are used for stool-seats, cushions and bags. Wool, silk, or cotton threads may be used.

Hessian   This is made of jute, and good bold designs can be worked on it, using fairly thick threads. Beach and shoe-bags and gardening aprons are articles that can be made from it.

Synthetic fabrics are often indistinguishable from fabrics made from natural fibres and can be used for the same purposes.

STITCHES

These are many and various, but excellent effects may be obtained from the use of very few. It is worth while spending some time practising and perfecting a limited number of stitches. The following list should be enough to begin with (*see* Fig. 282).

1. Running-stitch.	6. Blanket-stitch.
1a. Threaded running-stitch.	6a. Spaced blanket-stitch.
1b. Whipped running-stitch.	6b. Vandyke blanket-stitch.
2. Stem-stitch.	7. Feather-stitch.
3. Back-stitch.	7a. Double feather-stitch.
4. Chain-stitch.	8. Herringbone stitch.
4a. Zigzag chain-stitch.	9. Fly-stitch.
4b. Single chain-stitch.	10. Couching.
5. Satin-stitch.	

Experiment with these stitches, using them in different ways and positions. Some of them are essentially filling stitches, e.g. satin stitch, but others can be used for the same purpose. Running-stitch, blanket-stitch and single chain-stitch can all be used to fill spaces; so can couching. All give quite different effects. Some stitches used for outlining give a clear, firm line, while others give a feathery effect, quite altering the character of the work.

To start

To finish

FIG. 282

DESIGN

It is well worth while doing embroidery, even if you have no gift for design, but it is fun to try making your own designs, and there is great satisfaction in being able to say of a piece of work, "I designed it myself." The simplest way to begin designing is to use checked or striped material. Spotted material also lends itself to this type of designing. Embroider circles or stars in the squares and connect them with diagonal lines. Outline some of the squares and block out others completely. Vary the density of your design by varying your

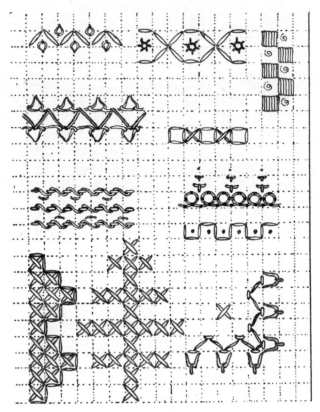

FIG. 283

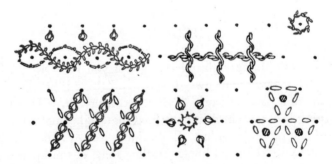

FIG. 284

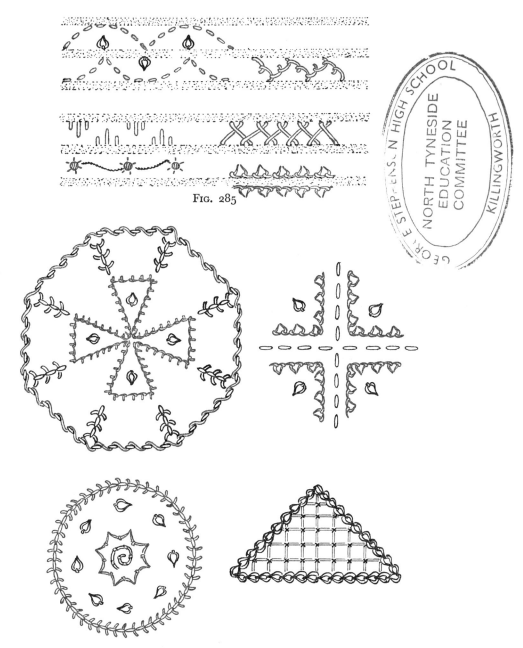

FIG. 285

Stitches fitted to simple geometrical shapes to form
designs

FIG. 286

125

stitches. Fill the spaces between the stripes with curved or zigzag lines. Connect the spots with lines of embroidery or use the spots as a basis for geometrical or flower-shaped motifs (*see* Figs. 283, 284, 285, 286).

Fig. 287   Fig. 288

Free stitchery is another simple method of designing. The stitches are used in rows or blocks to form narrow borders (*see* Figs. 287, 288, 289, 290). Cut

Fig. 289   Fig. 290

paper is another aid to designing; either cut a single motif and arrange it as desired (*see* Figs. 291, 292), or fold a strip of paper into eight and cut the edges

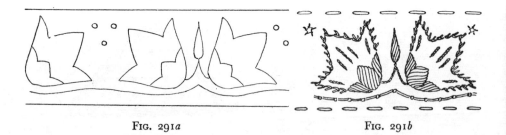

Fig. 291*a*   Fig. 291*b*

and folds so that when it is opened out you have a decorative border. Do not be too elaborate with your cutting or you will find it difficult to fit stitches to your design (*see* Fig. 293).

Fig. 292

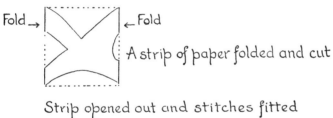

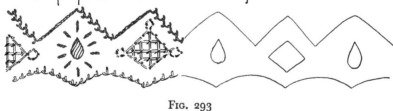

Fig. 293

MAKING AND TRANSFERRING DESIGNS

Border (using a single motif)

(*a*) Draw two lines, to give the required width of border.

(*b*) Cut out motif of suitable size in stiff paper or card.

(*c*) Arrange one section of your design, adding lines and curves where needed.

(*d*) Using a strip of tracing-paper of the correct width and length of the border, trace off the design, connecting the sections (*see* Fig. 291*a*).

(*e*) Decide on suitable stitches and colours. It helps if, at this stage, you draw in the stitches on the original section (*see* Fig. 291*b*).

(*f*) Transfer the design to the material by placing carbon paper between the tracing and the material. If the design is on tissue paper, it can be tacked firmly to the material and the embroidery done through the paper.

If the design is very simple, and has not to be repeated, it is possible to draw it straight on to the material, using a template of the motif.

Border (using a folded and cut strip)

(*a*) Using a strip of paper of the correct width and length, fold in eight and cut the design.

(*b*) Open strip out flat and hold firmly in place between the guide-lines on the tracing-paper.

(*c*) Trace off and add lines, curves and dots as required (*see* Fig. 293).

COLOUR

The choice of colour can make a tremendous difference to the design; it can make it stand out or appear insipid. Bold and exciting, or subtle colour in embroidery is always admired.

It is a mistake to use too many colours, as this tends to result in a confused effect. Three colours are usually sufficient and excellent results are achieved by using only one colour, particularly if the background is coloured. Do not be afraid of using black; a little black helps to make other colours stand out. White, too, can add life to a colour scheme. Colours may be either in harmony or in contrast.

Harmonizing colours always contain a common colour, for instance, green and orange harmonize because both contain yellow. The greatest contrast to any colour is one that contains none of the colours of which it is itself composed; for example, violet and yellow are contrasting colours. When using two colours together, whether they are in harmony or in contrast, a better and more pleasing result is obtained if a deep tone of one colour is used with a pale tone of the other; e.g., burnt orange with pale leaf green, or golden yellow with pale lilac.

SMOCKING

Smocking is a decorative way of controlling fullness. The fullness is held in place by embroidery stitches, and the work can vary in depth from 1 cm to several centimetres. The material used must be thin and soft; and stranded cotton, Coton-à-broder, and Filoselle are the most suitable threads for this work.

It is used most frequently on clothes for babies and small children, but it can also be used on nightdresses and the shoulders of blouses. Check gingham is a good material to experiment on, and very pleasing results can be obtained.

If you have bought a pattern on which smocking is shown, there should be a transfer covered with evenly spaced dots, inside the envelope. This transfer is essential if you are smocking on any material other than check gingham.

PREPARATION OF CHECK MATERIAL (*see* Fig. 294)

1. Working on the W.S. of the material run a gathering thread along the horizontal lines of the checks, picking up only two threads with your needle, where the vertical lines cross the horizontal lines.

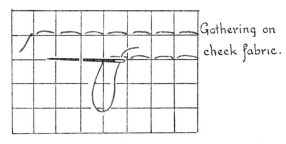

Gathering on check fabric.

FIG. 294

2. Work the required number of rows of gathering, starting each row strongly, and leaving the cotton hanging at the other end.

3. Pull the threads up in pairs to the required size; usually about one third of the original length; tie off each pair.

Looking at the work from the R.S. you should have a series of vertical pleats (*see* Fig. 295).

Gathering threads pulled up

FIG. 295

PREPARATION OF PLAIN MATERIAL (*see* Fig. 296)

1. Place your material R.S. down on the ironing board, and iron out flat.

2. While the material is still warm, place your transfer in position, with the shiny side of the transfer against the material. Pin the transfer to the material outside the dotted area.

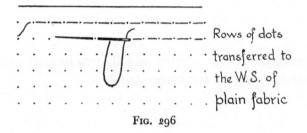

Preparation for Smocking

Rows of dots transferred to the W.S. of plain fabric

FIG. 296

3. Using a fairly warm iron, press (not iron) the transfer onto the material holding the iron in position for a second or two before moving it to a fresh place.

4. Gather along the lines of dots.

STITCHES (*see* Fig. 297)

Work on the R.S. starting from the left on the row of gathers below the fitting line.

Outline stitch is worked in the same way as stem stitch picking up one pleat each time, and always keeping the thread on the same side of the needle (*see* Fig. 297*a*).

Cable stitch is worked by picking up one pleat at a time, with the thread above the needle for the first stitch and below for the next (*see* Fig. 297*b*).

Wave stitch is worked upwards keeping the thread below the needle, and downwards with the thread above the needle (*see* Fig. 297*d*).

Diamond stitch is made on two rows of gathers, twisting the thread round each pleat as you move from one row to the other (*see* Fig. 297*f*).

Honeycomb stitch is made by placing the needle in the first pleat from

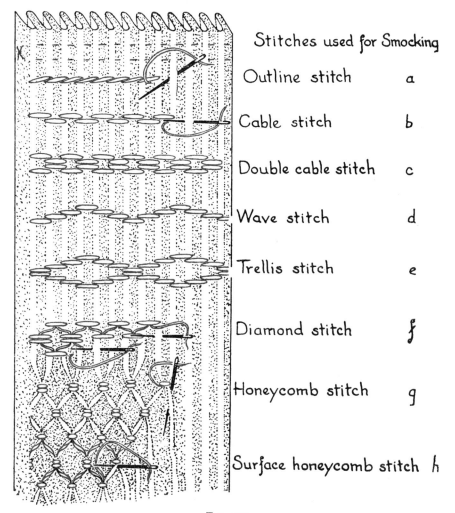

Stitches used for Smocking

Outline stitch   a

Cable stitch   b

Double cable stitch   c

Wave stitch   d

Trellis stitch   e

Diamond stitch   f

Honeycomb stitch   g

Surface honeycomb stitch   h

FIG. 297

R. to L. and in the second pleat in the same manner; by drawing the two pleats together and slipping the needle down inside the pleat to the next row of gathers, repeating the process, drawing the third pleat close to the second; finally the needle is taken up to the original line (*see* Fig. 297g).

Surface honeycomb stitch is worked in the same manner, but twisting the hread round the pleat instead of slipping it inside (*see* Fig. 297h).

APPLIQUÉ WORK

This is a method of decoration achieved by sewing one piece of material on another to form a pattern. It is not difficult to do and gives scope for originality in design and working. Almost any fabric can be used but care must be taken to ensure that the fabric being applied is about the same weight as the background material, as a heavier material would tend to tear away. Fabrics that fray badly should be avoided, though the difficulty of using such a fabric can be

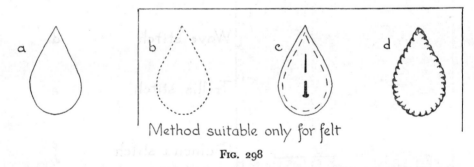

Method suitable only for felt

Fig. 298

overcome to some extent by using a thin adhesive backing on the applied material. The shapes that make up the design should be as simple as possible, as this helps to give the bold effect that is typical of appliqué work. The easiest material to use, and therefore the best one to begin with, is felt and very pleasing effects can be obtained.

METHOD FOR FELT (*see* Fig. 298)

1. Decide on your design and transfer it to the background. Embroider all connecting lines, using suitable stitches, such as stem-stitch for stems.

2. Transfer the solid shapes, such as leaves and flowers, to the material that is to be applied, and cut them out with sharp scissors. Embroider veins or markings.

3. Arrange the shapes on the design, pin and tack into position.

4. Work round the edge of each shape to fix it to the background, using a suitable stitch, such as blanket-stitch, running-stitch, fly-stitch. Coton-à-broder or stranded cotton are suitable threads.

Method Used for Materials Other Than Felt (*see* Fig. 299)

1. Transfer the design to the material to be applied and embroider veins, markings, etc. (*see* Fig. 299*a*).

2. Tack firmly into position on background material (*see* Fig. 299*b*).

3. If the material is slippery or otherwise difficult to handle, outline the design with tiny running-stitches through both layers of fabric.

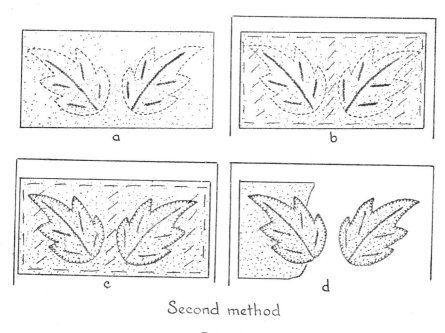

Second method

Fig. 299

4. Work round each shape, using very fine blanket- or satin-stitches (*see* Fig. 299*c*).

5. Cut away surplus material close to the stitches (*see* Fig. 299*d*). Use a thread of suitable weight for the fabric.

20

Lingerie

THERE are many useful and decorative processes suitable for underwear.

LACE

This is a pretty and popular trimming for underwear and nightwear. Lace is usually made from cotton or nylon and although as a general rule it is correct to use cotton lace on cotton materials and nylon lace on nylon and other man-made fabrics, it is wiser to use nylon lace on the non-iron lingerie fabrics, such as cotton plissé and seersucker, because nylon lace needs no ironing, and cotton lace does.

The design on lace is on the R.S., which makes it feel slightly more rough on that side.

Lace for edging can be bought in a variety of widths and in several colours. It has one straight edge and one shaped edge and there is usually a thread

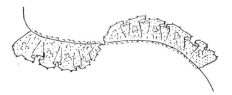

FIG. 300

running through the straight edge, which can be used to gather the lace (*see* Fig. 300).

Lace can also be obtained with both edges alike, either straight or shaped, again in varying widths, and this is called insertion lace. Piece-lace is the third type, and this is used to make complete garments or parts of garments, such as yokes.

Lace and net are not woven but knotted; therefore they have no grain and do not fray.

ATTACHING LACE TO EDGES

By Machine

(*a*) Tack and press a very narrow hem on the edge of the garment.

(*b*) Tack the lace to the R.S. of the hem in such a way that one row of machining holds both hem and lace in position. A more decorative effect may be obtained by using the zigzag attachment on the machine (*see* Fig. 301).

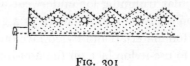

FIG. 301

By Whipping or Oversewing

(*a*) Neaten the edge of the garment with a narrow hem.

(*b*) If the lace is to be frilled, draw it up the required amount, using the thread already in the lace.

(*c*) Place the R.S. of the lace to the R.S. of the edge and pin into position, arranging the gathers evenly and allowing a little extra fullness on corners and curves.

(*d*) Whip the two edges together with tiny stitches, closely worked.

(*e*) Lift the lace and flatten the seam (*see* Fig. 302).

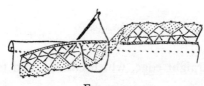

FIG. 302

By Using an Embroidery Stitch

(*a*) Place W.S. of the lace to the R.S. of the garment, with the straight edge of the lace about 0·5 cm in from the raw edge. Hold in position with running stitches.

(*b*) Using a fine embroidery thread, blanket-stitch closely along the edge of the lace (*see* Fig. 303).

(*c*) If the material is closely woven and does not fray, the surplus material

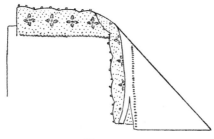

FIG. 303

may be cut away close to the back of the blanket-stitching. If the material is inclined to fray, roll and whip the raw edges.

Attaching Lace with Faggotting

Herringbone

(*a*) Neaten the edge of the garment with a narrow hem. Press.

(*b*) Tack the edge to a strip of paper.

(*c*) Tack the lace to the paper, leaving a 0·5 cm gap between the two edges.

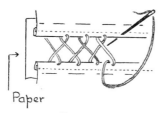

FIG. 309

(*d*) Using a fine embroidery thread, begin at the left side with a small back-stitch. Moving 3 mm to the R., and with the needle pointing L., take a small stitch in the edge of the lace. Moving 3 mm to the R., again take a small stitch in the edge of the garment; the second stitch should cross the first one.

(*e*) Continue in this manner, keeping the stitches evenly spaced (*see* Fig. 304).

Bar Faggotting

Prepare as for previous method.

(*a*) Beginning on the R., make a back-stitch in the hem and then a straight stitch, joining the two edges.

(*b*) Twist the needle twice round this stitch and then into the fold; slip the

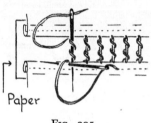

FIG. 305

needle along the fold to the position of the next stitch and repeat, spacing stitches evenly (*see* Fig. 305).

Faggotting may be used to join seams, or to attach bands or rouleau to edges.

LACE INSERTION

(*a*) Place the W.S. of the lace on the R.S. of the fabric in the required position and tack firmly.

(*b*) If the edges are straight they may be held in place by machining, but if the edges are shaped it is necessary to use blanket-stitch or satin-stitch.

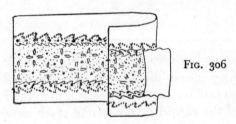

FIG. 306

(*c*) Cut away the fabric from the back of the insertion, either close to the embroidery stitches or leaving enough to roll and whip (*see* Fig. 306). Use the same method for inserting lace medallions.

JOINING LACE

(*a*) Place two pieces of lace so that the motif on one is on top of a similar motif on the other.

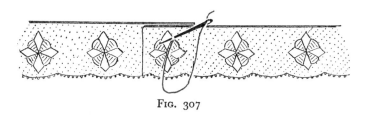

FIG. 307

(*b*) Using a very fine matching thread (if the lace has been gathered, use the end that has been pulled out), whip the two layers of lace together with tiny stitches, following the outline of the motif.

(*c*) Trim away the surplus lace on both sides of the work (*see* Fig. 307).

For methods of fixing narrow hems *see* page 91.

EMBROIDERY ON LINGERIE

Lingerie materials are usually fine and soft, and are often transparent; e.g. lawns, nylons and silks, and therefore the threads used must be fine. Stranded cottons and silks are suitable because they can be divided to suit the weight of the material. Crêpes and satins can be embroidered by the usual method, using any of the embroidery stitches, but transparent materials need special treatment. All stitches will show through and therefore the part that is usually invisible must help to create a pattern, as in shadow work. All ends must be invisibly secured. Avoid unnecessary joins by using a sufficiently long thread.

SHADOW-WORK

The design for this work should be chosen carefully, as the stitch used is worked more easily on symmetrical shapes.

This stitch is double back-stitch, which is closed herringbone on the reverse side. The best results are obtained by using a thread of a deeper shade than the

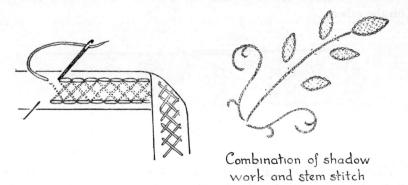

Combination of shadow
work and stem stitch

FIG. 308

material. Each motif or shape in the design is then outlined with back-stitches, and the closed herringbone shows through slightly paler than the outline. A pleasing and dainty effect is obtained (*see* Fig. 308).

SHADOW APPLIQUÉ WORK

(*a*) Transfer the design to the material.

(*b*) Tack a piece of material of a deeper shade behind the design (*see* Fig. 309*a*).

(*c*) Work tiny running-stitches round the solid shapes through both layers of material.

(*d*) Outline the shapes with closely worked blanket-stitch or satin-stitch in thread matching the backing material (*see* Fig. 309*a*).

(*e*) With sharp-pointed embroidery scissors, trim away the backing material close to the stitches (*see* Fig. 309*b*, *c*).

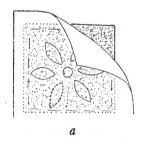 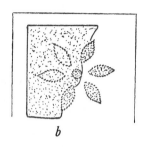 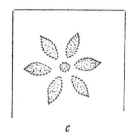

a   b   c

Fig. 309

MACHINE-QUILTING

This work is most effective on plain materials and is often used on bed-jackets and the collars and cuffs of housecoats and dressing-gowns. A sheet of wadding or flannel and a piece of thin, soft cotton, the same size as the material to be quilted, will be needed. A quilting foot on the machine is a great help, but the work can be done without.

For machine-quilting the design is made up of straight lines, squares or diamonds.

(*a*) Put the three layers of material together, sandwiching the wadding between the other two.

(*b*) Tack firmly together with rows of diagonal tacking, keeping all three layers perfectly smooth and flat.

(*c*) Mark the first line of stitching on the R.S. of the material and machine on the mark.

(*d*) The succeeding rows are made at even distances from one another. The guide on the quilting foot is a great help when doing this. If no quilting foot is available, then each row must be measured and marked.

(*e*) Complete all the lines going one way before beginning those running at right-angles.

(*f*) Press on the W.S. on a very soft cloth.

If the quilting is required for collars and cuffs, it is better to quilt a piece of material and then put your pattern on and cut out.

21

Repairs

ALTHOUGH the advent of man-made fibres has reduced the amount of mending to be done, the necessity still arises sometimes. The elbows of cardigans and jerseys still wear thin and so do the heels of socks. Garments are accidentally torn. The life of household articles such as sheets and table-cloths can be lengthened by mending them when they first show signs of wear.

DARNING

This is a suitable method of repairing thin places and small holes.
Darning should be done on the W.S. of the garment or article.
Match your thread (colour, fibre and thickness).
Use a needle long enough to span the darn if possible.
Repair a thin place before it wears into a hole.
When darning a hole, take the darn well into the unworn part of the garment.
Keep the garment taut but not stretched, and if darning by machine use an embroidery frame to hold the work.
Make your darn as invisible as possible.

THE STOCKING DARN

This type of darn is used to mend holes and thin places in garments made from machine- or hand-knitted fabrics.

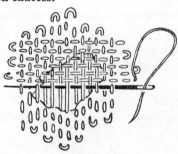

FIG. 310

142

1. Weave in and out of the threads of the fabric with small stitches, beginning in the direction of the loops and making a stitch into each loop.

2. Take your thread straight across the hole if there is one. If there is no hole, darning in one direction may suffice but if there is a hole, weave in and out at right angles to the first stitches, filling the hole as shown in the diagram.

3. Do not pull the threads tightly and do not fasten off.

4. If using a woollen thread, leave small loops at the end of every line of stitches as the thread may shrink (*see* Fig. 310).

THE CROSS-CUT DARN

This darn is more often needed on table-linen than anywhere else, and therefore a fine needle and thread are used. There is no worn area. A cross-cut is a diagonal one, not on the grain of the material.

1. Start and finish 1 cm beyond the end of the cut, and about the same distance either side.

2. Darn on the straight grain of the fabric, beginning in the direction of the warp threads.

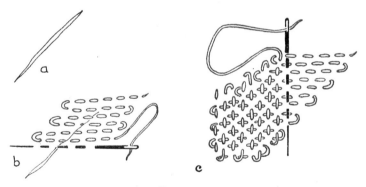

FIG. 311

3. The cut edges must be held together and kept quite flat.

4. When the darn is completed in this direction, weave across in the direction of the weft threads (*see* Figs. 311*a*, *b*, *c*).

This darn can be done very successfully on table linen with a darning attachment on the sewing-machine.

THE HEDGE-TEAR DARN

This darn is used to mend a right-angle tear on the grain of the fabric, where there is no worn area. The edges of the tear must be held together with fish-bone stitch (*see* Fig. 312*a*).

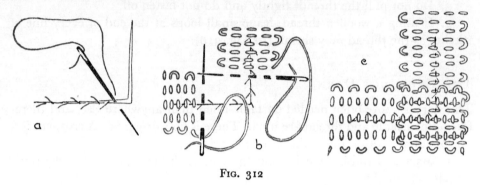

FIG. 312

1. Starting 1 cm beyond the end of one arm of the tear, darn on the straight grain and work across the tear until a point 1 cm beyond the angle of the tear is reached.

2. Starting 1 cm beyond the end of the other arm of the tear, darn on the cross grain to 1 cm beyond the angle, weaving in and out of the first threads, making a neat square and strengthening the corner (*see* Fig. 312*a*, *b*, *c*).

If it is possible to use a thread of the material to work with, the darn can be almost invisible.

PATCHING

Large holes and extensive worn places cannot be satisfactorily darned, so they must be patched. There are four different types of patches, each suited to its own special purpose. Always use material of the same weight and colour as the article to be patched. If new material is to be used for patching, wash it before using it. The patch must be large enough to take in all the worn area, or else the strain on the worn material will make it break away very quickly. If the hole is near a seam or hem, these must be unpicked before you begin to patch and re-sewn afterwards.

The Household or Calico Patch

This is the strongest patch of all and is used on bed-linen, men's pyjamas and overalls.

1. Cut the patch on the straight grain, either square or rectangular, and of the required size, allowing 0·5 cm turnings all round.

2. Press all turnings to the R.S. and mitre the corners. Place the patch in position on the W.S. of the garment, with the grain matching.

3. Working on a flat surface, pin and tack the patch into place.

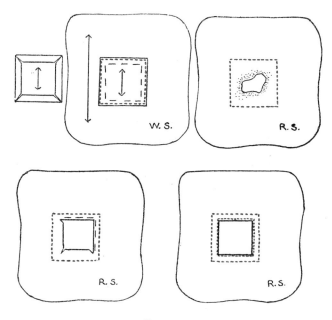

Fig. 313

4. Machine all round, close to the edge.
5. Cut away the worn material to 1 cm from the line of stitching.
6. Snip 0·5 cm into each corner and fold the raw edge under.
7. Pin, tack and machine close to the fold (*see* Fig. 313).

The Print Patch

This patch is not quite as strong as the calico patch, because it is held in place by only one row of stitching. It is done on the R.S. of the garment and is used on all printed and patterned materials.

    1. Cut the patch the required size, plus 0·5 cm turnings. The pattern must match that of the garment exactly, making the finished patch almost invisible.

    2. Press all turnings to the W.S. and mitre the corners. Place in position on the R.S. of the garment, with pattern and grain matching.

    3. Pin, tack and oversew all round.

    4. Trim away worn material to 0·5 cm from stitching.

    5. Blanket-stitch the two raw edges together (*see* Fig. 314).

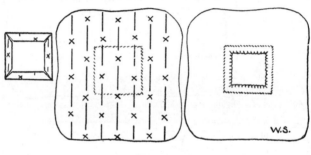

Fig. 314

The Flannel Patch

This is a strong, flat patch used on fine woollen materials and machine-knitted fabrics such as those used for underwear.

    1. Cut the patch to the required size, without turnings and on the same grain for woven materials, and with the loops in the same direction for knitted fabrics. Round off the corners.

    2. Place the patch in position on the W.S. of the garment and tack.

    3. Herringbone the patch to the garment.

    4. Trim away the worn material to 0·5 cm and herringbone to the patch (*see* Fig. 315).

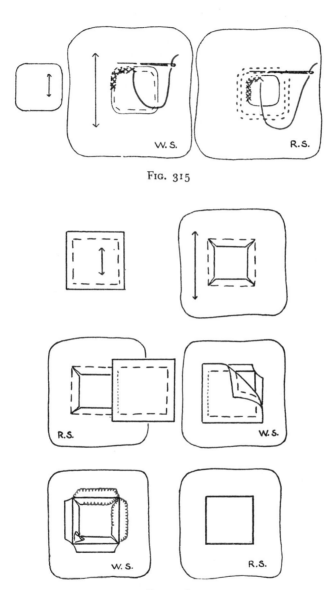

FIG. 315

FIG. 316

THE CLOTH PATCH

This patch is used on outer garments and is quite inconspicuous.

1. Cut a paper pattern the size of the patch required.

2. Mark the size of the patch on the garment with tacking, and cut away the worn part to within 1 cm of the tacking. Snip diagonally into the corners.

3. Cut the patch on the same grain as the garment, allowing 1 cm turnings.

4. Place the R.S. of one edge of the patch to the R.S. of the garment along one edge of the hole, with raw edges together.

5. Tack and back-stitch (from garment side) from corner to corner.

6. Pass the patch through the hole, turn the work to the W.S. and tack the remaining sides of the patch to the sides of the hole, with raw edges together.

7. Back-stitch each side, taking special care to keep the corners square and flat.

8. Trim the surplus material from the corners, press the seams open and blanket-stitch to neaten (*see* Fig. 316).

A TORN POCKET CORNER

1. Unpick the corner of the pocket.

2. Tack a piece of tape or matching material behind the tear.

3. Darn the torn edges on to the backing-piece.

4. Remove tacks and press.

5. Stitch pocket back to its original position.

A HOLE IN A STRETCH NYLON GLOVE

1. With matching nylon thread, blanket-stitch round the hole.

2. Work more rows of blanket-stitch into the loops of the previous row until the hole is filled.

RENOVATIONS

It is sometimes necessary to alter a garment, either because the figure or the fashion has changed, or because the garment has worn in certain parts.

Hem Alterations

The hem must be undone and the mark pressed out before either shortening (see page 86 for levelling and turning up hems) or lengthening by means of a false hem (*see* Fig. 188, page 91).

Seam Alterations

The whole length of the seam must be unpicked and pressed flat and the new seam pinned into place on the figure. In the case of the shoulder seam, the sleeve and neck finish must be removed first of all. If the alteration includes any re-cutting, the R. and L. sides must be pinned together before cutting.

To Shorten Sleeves

Remove the cuff and press lower edges of sleeves. Pin both sleeves together and cut off the required amount, keeping the end of the sleeve the same shape. Replace cuff, using method most suitable for style (*see* pages 100–103).

To make a dress worn at the underarm and neck into a pinafore dress unpick armhole seam and remove neck finish. Press all edges flat. Pin underarm seams together and shoulder seams together. Pin round armhole and neck edge. Re-cut to desired shape. If sleeves are large enough, cut neck and armhole facings from them or use a suitable braid to finish the neck and armholes.

22
Making the Best of Yourself

Time goes very quickly and one day in the not very far distant future you will be going for an interview, either for a college place or for a job. Your qualifications are, of course, extremely important, but the person who interviews you is a trained and experienced observer and he or she will be considering your poise, your interest and enthusiasm, and your appearance.

If you know that you are looking your best you will be self-confident and easy, and you can be sure that your well-groomed appearance will make a good impression.

What is good grooming? It means making the best of yourself in every detail. It is something that has to be worked at until it becomes a habit— quite a pleasurable habit, and one that every girl should acquire.

Your Figure

School uniform hides a multitude of bulges, and so do straight shift dresses, so strip off your clothes and be honest with yourself: Are you as streamlined as you would like to be? If not, then the remedy is to cut out those bars of chocolate, biscuits, crisps and buns that you eat between meals. Stop eating fried foods, particularly chips. Eat salads, eggs, cheese and lean meat instead. Be firm in refusing sweet cakes and puddings; raw fruit will do your figure and your complexion more good. If you are seriously overweight get help from your doctor.

Your Posture

The effect of a pretty face and smart clothes can easily be spoiled if you do not hold yourself well and move easily and gracefully. Poise and self-confidence are the natural result of standing, walking and sitting correctly—you will also be less tired at the end of the day.

Look at yourself sideways in a long mirror, your weight should not be on your heels but on the balls of your feet, and your knees should be straight but relaxed. Flatten your tummy and tuck your bottom in, let your shoulders relax and draw them back so that your back is nice and straight but not stiff. Hold your neck straight so that your head does not poke forward. Walk tall without bending from the waist or hips. When you sit use the whole of the chair seat and let the back support your spine. Keep your legs together and when you are writing bend forward from your hips not your shoulders.

Your Skin

The diet that helps to keep your figure in good shape will also help to keep your skin clear and healthy. Dairy products—milk, cheese, eggs and butter with lots of fresh fruit, salad and green vegetables, a reasonable proportion of cereals, bread and potatoes (not chips), meat and fish (provided they have not been fried) all add up to a balanced diet, which will help to keep your skin clear and unblemished.

Some skins are too dry and some are too greasy, but quite a large proportion of people are greasy around the nose, mouth and chin but dry on the cheeks and forehead.

Most young skins are naturally beautiful and do not look as if they need much outward attention, but a little care now will help to preserve its youthfulness.

Whether you wear make-up or not you should wash your face thoroughly before going to bed. Using luke-warm water and a good complexion soap, massage your face and neck gently with your fingers, rinse well and pat your skin dry with a soft towel using upward movements rather than downward ones. Some make-up is waterproof and washing may not remove it, so go over your face and neck with a pad saturated in cleansing milk and then remove surplus cleansing lotion with a clean tissue. If your skin is greasy follow up the cleansing routine by patting on a toning lotion which will close the pores and tighten the muscles, but if your skin is dry a moisturizing lotion instead of the toning lotion will be more beneficial. Remove surplus lotion before going to bed.

Some young people are plagued and made quite miserable by spots and blackheads. These are most common with greasy skins. The grease attracts dirt and the pores become blocked, the bacteria in the dirt sets up inflammation and you have an angry and unsightly spot.

Here are some hints on how to get rid of spots—

1. Don't squeeze or pick the spot.

2. Use a medicated soap which contains an antiseptic, and keep it for your own use.

3. Wash your hair often and keep it away from your face whether this is fashionable or not.

4. Use a greaseless ointment and after-wash lotion obtainable from the chemist to thoroughly clean and heal the spots.

Do not expect an overnight miracle cure, but if you persevere you will get results. The main thing is to watch your diet and lead an active life. Avoid greasy, fatty foods and spend as much time as possible in the fresh air. Use very little make-up on your skin until the condition has cleared.

For the whole of your school life your teeth have been examined regularly and you have had dental appointments whenever they have been needed. This excellent habit preserves your teeth and does away with one of the reasons for unpleasant breath, but there are other causes of bad breath. It can be caused by an upset tummy or by eating strongly-flavoured foods like onions or garlic. Clean your teeth and rinse your mouth after every meal, and if you are at all doubtful about the sweetness of your breath use a chlorophyl breath sweetener—they are very effective as a temporary measure.

Daily bathing or showering is essential if you are to be a nice person to be near. Personal hygiene must go further than washing if good grooming is your aim, and there is such a wide range of deodorants in several forms available at chemists and on cosmetic counters that there should be no difficulty in finding one that suits you. The regular use of deodorants and anti-perspirants can save you embarrassment and increase your self-confidence. Preventing perspiration in the parts of the body where it is offensive does no harm at all, and anti-perspirants can be used without fear.

This care of your body is specially necessary during your monthly periods, and there are several excellent products which can help you very effectively over these tiresome days. All such products are advertised extensively, so it is easy to find out about them.

MAKE-UP

We use make-up to make us more attractive, but because there are fashions in make-up it is necessary to be selective and resist the extremes that only look right under brilliant stage lighting. Choose your make-up so that it suits your type of skin (dry or greasy) and your natural colouring.

Most foundation lotions or creams are non-greasy and contain a moisturizer and are obtainable tinted or colourless. They form a protective film against weather and dirt. Choose a tint that blends with your natural colouring and match it with loose powder and a compact for touching up.

Use your foundation sparingly, smoothing it evenly over your face and neck, apply the loose powder liberally with cotton wool, pressing it onto your skin, then dust off the surplus. If you need colour, apply the blusher (powder rouge) with a very light touch being careful not to leave a line. Brush the powder from your eyebrows and eyelashes, and define your eyebrows with a well-pointed eyebrow pencil using short strokes—don't use a black pencil unless you are very dark.

Eye shadow makes your eyes look larger, choose a colour that accentuates the colour of your eyes and apply it lightly being careful not to stretch the skin. Mascara is waterproof, so if you buy it get the remover at the same time; if you are fair, brown or blue mascara looks more natural than black. False eyelashes are fine for evening wear but you will need practice in putting them on.

Soft pink lipstick is prettier and more natural than red, and a slightly orange-toned lipstick looks well with a sun-tanned skin. You get a better line if you put your lipstick on with a brush. Be very careful not to go over the edge, blot your lips with a tissue and apply another coat. Keep the make-up that you carry round with you in its own bag, not loose in your handbag.

Your Hair

It is an old saying that hair is "a woman's crowning glory", but a true one only if the hair is healthy and well cared-for. Cleanliness of hair and scalp is essential, and it does no harm to wash your hair two or three times a week to keep the shining, silken look. Use a shampoo recommended for your type of hair and soft or softened water that is not too hot. Most makes of shampoo are available for normal, greasy or dry hair, but if your hair is exceptionally dry you may need to use a conditioner to make it more manageable.

Opinions have changed about the desirability of brushing hair, some experts say that combing is sufficient and that excessive brushing activates the oil glands of the scalp and makes the hair greasy. In any case, a pure bristle brush is much kinder than a nylon one. Remember to wash your brush and comb every time you wash your hair.

Have your hair cut and styled to suit your face, and don't follow fashion slavishly. Long curtains of hair do not suit every face any more than a short crop does. Remember your hair is the frame for your face and it can either enhance or spoil the picture.

Well-cut hair is not difficult to set at home, using rollers if it is straight and needs a lift or, if it has a natural wave, finger setting and pin curls. There are setting lotions to suit all types of hair, but be careful in your choice of a hair spray. Avoid the sticky ones as they collect dirt. The good ones contain a conditioner which helps your hair to look soft and glossy.

If you have any problems, such as excessive loss of hair, or dandruff, ask your hairdresser if he can put you in touch with a Trichologist. You can do more harm than good by trying to treat it yourself.

Your Hands

Your hands are just as noticeable as your face and deserve as much, if not more, care.

File your nails to an oval shape with an emery board (it is much more gentle than a metal file). Rest each finger tip on a firm surface and file from the sides to the centre in one direction only.

Wash your hands using a good soap, and dig your nails into a soft soapy sponge to clean them, hard nail brushes can damage your nails. Use an orange stick to remove loosened dirt.

Push back your cuticles daily using an orange stick with a rubber end. Never use a metal instrument which can bruise the nail and damage its surface, and do not cut your cuticles or they will become ragged and untidy. Use a cuticle cream to soften the cuticle and feed the nail, then you will avoid brittle and broken nails.

Nail varnish can look very nice, but only if it is in perfect condition, so remove it with an oily remover at the first sign of a chip. Don't wear varnish continually; your nails will stay in better condition if you just buff them, except for special occasions. Unless you have long tapering fingers and beautifully shaped nails do not wear brightly coloured nail varnish, the paler opalescent colours are much more flattering to hands that are less than perfect.

If you bite your nails try to be strong-minded enough to break this unpleasant habit and start taking a pride in your hands. Protect your hands with gloves if you have a dirty job to do and use a good hand-cream after washing them.

Your Feet and Legs

We expect a great deal from our feet and rarely give them the attention they deserve.

Bathe your feet daily, dry them with an upward movement from toes to ankles and dust them with deodorizing foot powder. Keep your toenails trimmed and the cuticles pushed back. Watch for corns and callouses which are usually caused by pressure or rubbing, treat them and remove the cause. Rough and red heels are the result of badly fitting shoes so take great care when buying shoes to get the right size (length and width) and the style that suits the shape of your foot. Do not neglect your feet. If you think that there is anything wrong, get help from a chiropodist.

Clean stockings every day are a must and do make sure that they are not too short in the foot.

If you want to go bare-legged in the summer you must look after your legs all the year round. If they are hairy use a depilatory which will get rid of it and with regular use discourage the growth altogether; hand cream will keep the skin soft and smooth. Resist the temptation to sit too close to the fire in the winter; scorch marks are very unsightly and take a long time to fade.

Your Clothes

Modern lingerie is a joy to see and to wear. Underwear made from man-made, easycare fabrics are dainty, lightweight, strong, and they stand up well to constant washing. Bra, girdle, pantie and slip can be washed through daily as easily as stockings or tights and it is well worth the little extra trouble to have the healthy, fresh feeling that absolute cleanliness gives.

Use your knowledge of fabrics and how they behave in wear when choosing garments or the fabric for making garments. Will the garment look as fresh and uncreased when you get out of the car or bus as it did when you got in? Fabric manufacturers have helped so much in recent years by providing materials which are suitable for any kind of occasion and wear that there is no excuse for anyone to look creased and crumpled when either working or travelling.

Provided the right choice has been made it is possible to look as well groomed at the end of the day as at the beginning.

When buying light-coloured fabrics or garments do find out whether they will launder easily or need to be dry-cleaned and then treat them according to the instructions given so that they will keep their good appearance always. White can rarely be worn more than once without washing, this applies particularly to collars and cuffs so make sure that they are detachable and will wash easily.

Examine each garment when you take it off to see whether it is too soiled to wear again; look for loose buttons and fastenings and other small repairs and attend to them at once. Look also for spots that can be removed without washing or cleaning the whole garment. In fact, when you hang the garment up it must be ready to wear again. Most creases will fall out if garments are kept on hangers when not being worn. Keep jerseys and cardigans clean and folded in polythene bags. Your shoes and boots need cleaning and polishing every day, and do keep the heels in good repair as worn-down heels look slovenly and make you walk badly.

The hints and instructions in this chapter may sound like a lot of work but most worthwhile things take some effort to achieve. The result should be a poised, self-assured girl who is confident that she is looking her best.

23
Choosing the Right Clothes

Your physical characteristics and the type of life you lead, must be your strongest influences when choosing clothes for yourself. Study yourself carefully in front of a full-length mirror.

The shape of your face and the length of your neck make a lot of difference to the type of neckline that you can wear. If your face is round or your neck is short a vee neckline helps to give an illusion of length, but if your face is too long choose a boat-shaped neckline that cuts across. Long-necked people look particularly well in large collars that stand up round the neck.

Have you got square or sloping shoulders? If they slope, then flat necklines and small collars will suit you best, and you should avoid raglan sleeves, as the diagonal lines accentuate the slope. Square shoulders need the sort of collar that builds up the neckline; keep the armhole line smooth and unobtrusive.

A large bust can be made less obvious by choosing styles with vertical lines, such as a central opening set in a panel. Avoid breast-pockets and shoulder-yokes, or any styling that draws attention to the bust. Short sleeves should also be avoided as they tend to add width. The small or undeveloped bust can be helped by wearing styles that have fullness or draping falling from the neck or shoulder lines.

If your waist is small you have no problem. A large waist should not be accentuated by belts of contrasting colour, and your clothes should either by-pass your waist completely, as in boxy styles, or should be fitted smoothly over the waistline, with flat seams or darts to control the fullness, avoiding a waist seam altogether.

Small hips are generally considered an asset and they will not interfere with your choice of style, but if your hips are not slim, then bunchy skirts gathered or pleated into the waist are not for you. A shaped skirt, where the fullness is controlled by means of extra seams and darts, will suit you much better. Keep the line from your waist to below your hips smooth and let the fullness spring from below that line.

If you are very tall, choose styles that cut across your figure. Bold designs and contrasting materials, large collars and cuffs, can all look smart and suitable on you. If you are short, avoid these things and concentrate on verticle lines both in style and material.

Colour and texture play a large part in making or marring your clothes. Generally speaking, dark, dull-surfaced materials make you look smaller and slimmer, and light colours and glossy materials make you look larger. This does not mean that the big girl must never wear light colours, though she should avoid shiny materials, except possibly as trimmings. A completely white outfit would certainly make her look larger but she can look very smart in pale colours, provided she has chosen the style wisely.

Most young people can wear vivid colours successfully, but you should not wear more than one at a time; give point to it by teaming it with a neutral shade. Gay prints are youthful and attractive, but leave the large designs for the well-made girl and never wear two patterned materials together. A plain skirt and a patterned blouse, or vice versa, go well together; a printed dress with a jacket of one of the colours in the print looks attractive and right, but if you team a flowered blouse with a striped skirt the result is confused, and even though both materials are pretty and the colours harmonize, the general effect will not be good.

When using the word texture, which, strictly speaking, refers to the weave, we think of the "feel" and the appearance of the material, and this should be taken into account when choosing a garment. Soft, flimsy materials look charming on the slender girl, but if you are not really slim you will be well advised to choose more solid materials with a firmer "handle." Heavy, nobbly tweeds, and coatings with a very shaggy surface are not really suitable for the small person; she does better to choose a closely woven, smooth-surfaced material and to leave the rough ones for the bigger girl.

When you have decided what really suits you, go through your wardrobe and pick out the clothes that "do something for you," and let them form the nucleus of all your new purchases.

It helps a great deal if you decide on a basic neutral colour, such as grey, beige, brown, navy or black, whichever suits you best. Team it with your favourite colour and one other that harmonizes. Choose all your clothes from tones of these three colours and you will never find that you have an odd and useless garment in your wardrobe that does not "go" with anything else. Avoid impulse buying; you are sure to regret it.

Whatever type you are, remember that simplicity is another name for good taste and shun elaborate and fussy styles.

Give time and thought to planning your clothes; every outfit or combination of garments should make a pleasing impression. Each article of clothing should complement the others and you should be able to ring the changes with them so that you can have variety with reasonable economy. Do not attempt to follow extreme fashions; they are often short lived and therefore extravagant. Adapt the new trends to suit your own individual style and the results will be attractive as well as up to date. Try not to buy very cheap clothes; they lose their shape and their smartness very quickly. It is also well worth while to buy good quality materials if you make your own clothes, as they are much easier to work on, which in itself ensures better results.

It is important that you should choose the right clothes to wear on any given occasion; to be dressed wrongly can be both physically and mentally uncomfortable. Mentally, because you will be conscious that other people are criticizing your choice of clothes; for instance, if you wore stretch pants and a sweater to a formal party. Physically, the wrong clothes can make it difficult or impossible for you to join in the activities; a tight skirt and thin, high-heeled shoes will prevent you enjoying a country ramble.

Accessories should be chosen carefully, so that they can be used with more than one outfit. Buy the best you can afford, and if they are meant to match they must do so perfectly; but do not try to match everything, or the result will be very uninteresting.

Do not be lavish with jewellery; one piece, or at the most two, are quite sufficient and will highlight your outfit. One piece of quite cheap jewellery, provided that it is the right colour and shape, can look very pleasing and much more valuable than it really is. If, however, you wear an imitation brooch, necklace, ear-rings and bracelets, nobody will be deceived and the general effect will be spoiled.